Alpena Co. Library
211 N. First Ave.
Alpena, MI 49707

CONTROVERSY!

Government Entitlements

Jeff Burlingame

361.60973
BURL
C.1

Marshall Cavendish
Benchmark
New York

Copyright © 2012 Marshall Cavendish Corporation
Published by Marshall Cavendish Benchmark
An imprint of Marshall Cavendish Corporation

All rights reserved.
No part of this publication may be reproduced, stored in a retrieval system or transmitted, in any form or by any means, electronic, mechanical, photocopying, recording, or otherwise, without the prior permission of the copyright owner. Request for permission should be addressed to the Publisher, Marshall Cavendish Corporation, 99 White Plains Road, Tarrytown, NY 10591.
Tel: (914) 332-8888, fax: (914) 332-1888.
Website: www.marshallcavendish.us

This publication represents the opinions and views of the author based on Jeff Burlingame's personal experience, knowledge, and research. The information in this book serves as a general guide only. The author and publisher have used their best efforts in preparing this book and disclaim liability rising directly and indirectly from the use and application of this book.

Other Marshall Cavendish Offices:
Marshall Cavendish International (Asia) Private Limited, 1 New Industrial Road, Singapore 536196 • Marshall Cavendish International (Thailand) Co Ltd. 253 Asoke, 12th Flr, Sukhumvit 21 Road, Klongtoey Nua, Wattana, Bangkok 10110, Thailand • Marshall Cavendish (Malaysia) Sdn Bhd, Times Subang, Lot 46, Subang Hi-Tech Industrial Park, Batu Tiga, 40000 Shah Alam, Selangor Darul Ehsan, Malaysia

Marshall Cavendish is a trademark of Times Publishing Limited
All websites were available and accurate when this book was sent to press.

Library of Congress Cataloging-in-Publication Data
Burlingame, Jeff. • Government entitlements / Jeff Burlingame.
p. cm.—(Controversy!) • Includes bibliographical references and index.
Summary: "Allows readers to use critical thinking to create informed opinions on where they stand on the issue of government entitlement"—Provided by publisher.
ISBN 978-1-60870-491-0 (print) • ISBN 978-1-60870-643-3 (ebook)
Public welfare—United States—Juvenile literature. 2. Entitlement spending—United States Juvenile literature. 3. United States—Social policy—Juvenile literature. I. Title.
HV95.B78 2012 • 361.60973—dc22 • 2010046781

Publisher: Michelle Bisson • Art Director: Anahid Hamparian
Series Designer: Alicia Mikles • Photo research by Lindsay Aveilhe

The photographs in this book are used by permission and through the courtesy of:
Newscom: cover; Craig Fujii/AP Photo: p. 4; The Granger Collection: pp. 13, 22; Frank Wolfe/Bettmann/Corbis: p. 31; The Granger Collection: pp. 34, 39; Bettmann/Corbis: p. 47; Francis Miller/Time Life Pictures/Getty Images: p. 52; Bettmann/Corbis: p. 57; Chris Pfuhl/AP Photo: p. 65; Library of Congress/The Art Archive: p. 68; Peter Newark American Pictures/The Bridgeman Art Library International: p. 75; Win McNamee/Getty Images: p. 79; The Granger Collection: p. 85; Stock Connection Blue/Alamy: p. 90; Spencer Platt/Getty Images: p. 95; Margaret Bourke-White/Time & Life Pictures/Getty Images: p. 100; Todd Maisel/NY Daily News Archive via Getty Images: p. 103; Ed Kashi/Corbis: p. 106; Chris Hondros/Getty Images: p. 109; Newscom: p. 111; AFP Photo/Saul Loeb/Newscom: p. 115.

Printed in Malaysia (T)
135642

Contents

Introduction	5
1. Historical Overview	9
2. Social Security	35
3. Welfare	53
4. Unemployment Insurance	69
5. Workers' Compensation	81
6. Veterans Affairs	95
7. Miscellaneous Entitlement Programs	108
8. Conclusion	114
Notes	119
Further Information	132
Bibliography	134
Index	137

Whoopi Goldberg shown here arriving with her daughter, Alexandra Martin, at the 1991 Oscars, where Goldberg was nominated as best supporting actress for her role in the movie *Ghost*. As a teenager raising a child, Goldberg relied on government welfare and food stamps to stay alive and off the streets.

Introduction

CARYN ELAINE JOHNSON DROPPED OUT OF HIGH school at sixteen. Years later, she said, "I couldn't understand what they were doing . . . I just couldn't handle it." By eighteen, she was a strung-out junkie, captive both to the temporary "joy in a high" drugs gave her, and to the unrelenting desire to use drugs more frequently to obtain that elusive ecstasy. The following year, she had her first child.

Poorly educated and with a newborn child, Johnson let her longtime dream of becoming an actress lead her to California (She said, acting was "the one thing I always knew I could do") but, when she got there, could not find enough work to make ends meet. Reluctantly, she turned to the government for help.

For Johnson, better known today as Whoopi Goldberg, that help came from welfare, one of several entitlement programs the federal government had available to assist low-income Americans, or those without incomes, in times of need. As the term "entitlement" indicates, those who qualified for such programs had a legal *right* to receive governmental assistance. In Goldberg's case, that help came from the Aid to Families with Dependent Children program. That program has since been replaced by Temporary Assistance to Needy Families, which is not an entitlement program: that is, no one has an automatic right to its benefits.

Raised by a single black mother in a New York City housing project, Goldberg exemplified the social stereotype of the minority

Government Entitlements

single mom on welfare. She says that the five years during which she relied on that monthly check for survival produced many humiliating experiences. She told *Ebony* magazine in 1991 that her welfare caseworkers "used to make these surprise visits because you weren't allowed to have friends—especially not friends to whom you might want to be polite and *feed* something. If a welfare worker did surprise you and you happened to have a friend in the house with a plate of food in front of them, it would be deducted from your money the next month." Issues aside, Goldberg acknowledges that the program helped her through a rough time in life; she has no idea what would have happened to her without it. "The welfare system works," she says. "I know it works because I'm here. . . . I'm proud of it. The country was there for me, and the system worked for me."

Now an award-winning actress, comedian, and television talk show host, Goldberg has seen her welfare-to-riches story cited several times by politicians who also believe that government entitlement programs play an important role in American society and should continue to do so.

On the surface, it is difficult to argue against the case for government entitlement programs. The benefits of helping a fellow human through a tough time have been preached since the beginning of written history, and likely before. It simply seems to be the right thing to do. Someone falls down, another lends a hand to pick the person up. But in the hotly debated world of government entitlement programs, almost any decision related to extending that helping hand is highly controversial. There are many who do not believe such assistance should be available at all, at least not from the federal government.

U.S. congressional representative Ron Paul is one such person. The Texas Republican has spoken out several times against government involvement in social welfare of any type. In 2003, Paul said, "no one can deny that welfare programs have undermined America's moral fabric and constitutional system. Therefore, all

Introduction

those concerned with restoring liberty and protecting civil society from the maw of the omnipotent state should support efforts to eliminate the welfare state, or, at the very least, reduce federal control over the provision of social services."

Such antientitlement sentiments as Paul's have a long lineage. Benjamin Franklin, a founding father of the United States, frequently argued against the welfare policies of his day. Franklin believed it was up to individuals to provide for their own care because it was not government's responsibility to address their needs. He argued that those who did receive such assistance would develop dependence, become lazy and content, and never seek to better themselves. In 1753—as the United States was laying the social groundwork that would be written into its Constitution some thirty-five years later—Franklin wrote:

> I have sometimes doubted whether the laws . . . which compel the Rich to maintain the Poor have not given the latter a Dependence that very much lessens the care of providing against the wants of old Age. . . . To relieve the misfortunes of our fellow creatures is concurring with the Deity; it is Godlike but if we provide encouragements for Laziness, and supports for Folly, may it not be found fighting against the order of God and Nature, which perhaps has appointed Want and Misery as the proper Punishments for . . . Idleness and Extravagancy?

The issue of government entitlement is not only a social one. It is a financial one, as well. The services provided by entitlement programs are funded through taxes collected from working individuals who frequently disagree about how their hard-earned money should be used. It is obvious that tax funds dedicated to pay for one program should not be used to finance other programs. But should paying for the living expenses of a single mother and

7

Government Entitlements

her children take precedence over building new schools for those children and others? Should paying for the medical coverage of a low-income retired person be a higher priority than funding a study to find a cure for cancer that ultimately would benefit untold numbers of people? Seldom is the issue of what to do with tax revenue uncontroversial. There are also many who believe the government should have very little involvement in the lives of its citizens at all.

Exactly what role, if any, government should play in helping its needy citizens has been debated for centuries. Such discussions extend far beyond welfare. U.S. entitlement programs of all types are controversial: Social Security, unemployment insurance, veterans benefits, and many more.

1 Historical Overview

TO UNDERSTAND THE RATIONALE BEHIND ENTITLEMENT programs in the United States today, it is important to understand where those programs originated. The American social welfare system owes its basic structure to the English Poor Laws of the early seventeenth century, which in turn were based on customs of societies past. And so it goes throughout the ages and cultures, as far back as such practices can accurately be traced—that is, to some of history's earliest writings.

As ancient texts indicate, societies have long recognized the importance of taking care of their needier members. Egyptian writings dating back to more than 2,500 years before the Common Era tell of the help citizens received during the frequent periods when drought compromised the ability of the Nile River to supply the area's irrigation needs. One particularly gruesome text written by an Egyptian leader read: "When the entire Upper Egypt was dying because of hunger, with every man eating his (own) children, I never allowed death to occur from hunger in this [area]. I gave a loan of grain to Upper Egypt."

In the eighteenth century BCE, Babylonian king Hammurabi declared in his code of laws that "the strong might not injure the weak, in order to protect the widows and orphans. . . ." Some twelve hundred years later, the ancient Romans implemented a program they named *annona*, after the Roman goddess of the harvest. The program provided poor citizens with tokens, or *tesserae*, which they could exchange for basic food products such as corn or bread.

Government Entitlements

The program was later expanded to include lunch programs, or *alimenta*, for schoolchildren. The Romans' periodic counterparts, the Greeks, also strongly believed in charity. Indeed the English word *philanthropy* comes from a Greek expression for "friend of mankind." Greek philosopher Aristotle famously wrote that it was better to give than to receive, a saying that was paraphrased in the Bible and still is well known and widely repeated.

Many of the world's religions also preach the importance of helping others. Islam—a faith with more than a billion followers—teaches that all things on Earth belong to god and that humans are only temporarily in charge. The followers of Islam, called Muslims, are guided by the Five Pillars of Islam, one of which is the *zakat*, or the obligation to give alms to the poor. Islam's Prophet Muhammad said, "Charity is a necessity for every Muslim," and even if a person has no worldly possessions, "he should work with his own hands for his benefit and then give something out of such earnings in charity."

Judaism teaches that if someone lacks food, "he should be fed; if he needs clothing, he should be clothed; if he lacks household utensils, they should be purchased for him." Christianity, which today has more adherents than any other world religion, was built on the Hebrew belief of the obligation of Jews to care for the needy. Over time, Christians even placed extra emphasis on giving to the poor, saying it was better than either fasting or prayer. Other prominent religions of the world, such as Buddhism and Hinduism, hold similar beliefs about helping those in need. Buddhist monasteries, for example, have a long history of feeding the hungry in their respective regions, as well as taking in unwanted children, who are then usually brought up in the tradition and trained as monks or nuns.

Heavily influenced by religion, especially Christianity, Western European governments always have made some provisions for the needy. Years of disease, famine, social instability, and wars in

Historical Overview

England resulted in the implementation of Britain's Poor Laws, a series of acts that mandated assistance for needy people, including children, the able-bodied, and the disabled. The best-known legislation in this series was the Poor Law of 1601, also known as the Elizabethan Poor Law. The law—which was a written summary of the way England already had been treating its destitute for hundreds of years—guided England's policies on social welfare for more than two and a half centuries. Its basic principles included the following:

- A requirement that family members help support one another.
- A requirement for citizens to help neighbors in need.
- A work requirement for those who were not prevented from taking jobs by physical disability.
- The division of the poor into two categories: the "deserving" and the "undeserving." Those believed to deserve assistance included orphans and elderly, disabled, or sick people. Unmarried mothers, the able-bodied unemployed, and vagrants were among those held to be undeserving of aid.
- The taxing of every household to help pay for the relief of poverty.

American Colonies

Just a few years after the Elizabethan Poor Law was enacted, the first group of English explorers arrived on the eastern coast of North America in the area now known as Jamestown, Virginia. Although those one hundred English men and boys were not the first Europeans to reach the New World, theirs was the first permanent British settlement on the continent, and the history of the United States is often said to have begun in Jamestown. The Britons landed and settled in the midst of a large tribe of Indians with whom they

Government Entitlements

would soon go to war. Food in Jamestown was scarce, as were the skills needed to grow crops or raise livestock, so the settlers quickly established an important policy: "No work, no food."

Despite the early struggles at Jamestown, additional settlers came to the New World from England and many other countries. Included among them were the Pilgrims, who sailed aboard the *Mayflower* from England with a goal of landing in Virginia. The vessel drifted off course, however, and made landfall in modern-day Massachusetts. All who arrived in America hoped to capitalize on the abundance of natural resources that had been reported by explorers. Many people did just that, acquiring land and riches beyond imagination. Work was plentiful in the New World, and anyone who wanted a job generally could find one.

However, the majority of the English people who traveled to America prior to the 1680s came as indentured servants contracted to work for someone else for a set amount of time. These servants generally were poor, and their arrival in America did not mean a speedy escape from poverty. Soon, American colonies were forced to enact laws to provide for the care of their poor, elderly, sick, and destitute residents.

In the first session of its colonial legislature in 1647, Rhode Island adopted England's Poor Law as a way to take care of its own needy. Emphasis was placed on giving the public—the taxpayers—responsibility for the poor, although the government was not entirely out of the equation. The Rhode Island legislature said "that each towne should provide carefully for the relief of the poor, to maintain the disabled and to employ the able," and appoint an overseer for these purposes. Other colonies followed suit, and soon the New World was treating its poor, sick, and destitute in accordance with the Poor Laws of England. It was just as it had been in the Old World.

Some of the original governing methods employed by the colonies would today be considered strange, perhaps even inhumane. In

Historical Overview

Many of the early settlers in the thirteen colonies worked as indentured servants, as is shown in this engraving of a plumber and his servants.

Government Entitlements

1687, for example, one Massachusetts town ruled that a destitute widow should be sustained by spending two weeks at a time with any family in the town that was "able to receive her." At other times—because the needy received fixed payments, clothing, and medical care from their local government—the poor would be put up for bid at auction, with the lowest bidder winning, rather than the highest, as is usually the case. This was because the winning bidder had to fulfill certain humanitarian obligations. In one instance, that meant providing the needy person with "suitable Meats, and Drinks, Bedding mending, Nursing, & Tobacco if needed, the Bedding belonging to the poor is to go with them." In turn, the winning bidder was entitled to put the poor person to work as he saw fit.

Unemployed colonists were not looked upon favorably. Author Walter I. Trattner writes that "in the American colonies (as in England), voluntary idleness was regarded as a vice, and the able-bodied unemployed were either bound out as indentured servants, whipped and run out of town, or put in jail; in short, they were viewed not only as odious but as criminal, threats to themselves as well as to the entire community."

Almshouses were another means early settlers used to care for impoverished persons. These institutions sprang up in many colonial cities and towns, providing food, clothing, and shelter for those deemed in need of long-term assistance. Later, as the revolutionary era faded into history, almshouse-like facilities called poorhouses became the most popular way of caring for the poor in many areas. In Massachusetts in 1860, roughly 80 percent of the long-term poor resided in poorhouses. The quality of life in poorhouses varied; some residents were inadequately taken care of, while others were maintained in a respectable manner. Oftentimes, children who were deemed capable of learning a trade were sent to live with local families that could offer them such an opportunity as an alternative to staying in poorhouses. Needy children of the

Almshouses and Poorhouses

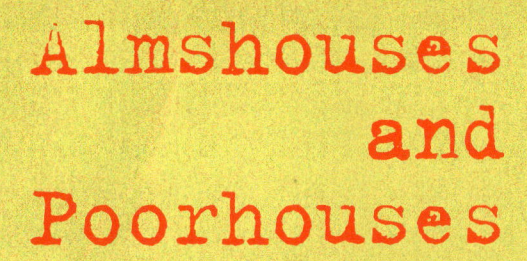

The housing of the less fortunate has taken various forms over many centuries. In early America, almshouses and poorhouses offered two of the most common types of care.

The giving of alms is a tradition in many religions. In its most basic sense it is the act of offering charity or assistance to someone less fortunate. Almshouses originally were founded during the Middle Ages to care for the elderly and the sick. Sometimes almshouses actually were hospitals, especially when the impoverished residents also had incurable diseases such as leprosy.

The oldest known almshouse is the Hospital of St. Cross, in England, which opened in the twelfth century and still is in operation today. The hospital's original mission was to house a small number of sick and injured men who were unable to work, and to feed poor people at its gates each day. In common with many other almshouses, this mission grew with the institution itself, and over the years farming and food preparation facilities were added and expanded, both to give the residents the dignity of daily work and to allow the hospital to broaden its outreach and feed more indigent people.

Poorhouses, on the other hand, were a nineteenth-century phenomenon that centered on the public perception that poor and homeless people were lacking in moral character. Some of these facilities took more benign forms, such as almshouses, but many were thinly disguised prisons, and residents were punished for breaking the rules. In the United States poorhouses were sometimes attached to "poor farms." Residents were expected to work on the farm and grow at least part of their own food.

There still are a large number of almshouses in Europe, most of them affiliated with religious orders. But the poorhouse concept largely died out in the United States after the passage of the Social Security Act in 1935. Facilities that house the homeless now generally do so on temporary terms and are referred to as "shelters."

Historical Overview

day frequently became apprentices under a skilled worker.

Although the Poor Laws in effect in early America were widely accepted and even popular, they often were challenged. Many people fundamentally opposed the concept of aiding down-on-their-luck individuals, especially if nothing was expected of the aid recipients. Benjamin Franklin wrote, "the support of the poor should not be by maintaining them in idleness, but by employing them in some kind of labour suited to their abilities of body."

There were exceptions and exemptions to the Poor Laws. In most of the American colonies, disabled sailors and soldiers were treated much better than those who had never served in the military; in fact, veterans continued to receive the same pay they had drawn while actively defending the colonies. They were seen as having earned the right to be taken care of. Their stipends came directly from the colonial governments, not from the individual towns, as was the case for other needy individuals.

The Poor Laws also did not apply to certain minority groups. American Indians, whom the English settlers considered to be savages, were forced out of developing colonial towns and onto infertile lands and federal reservations, where they were all but ignored by the colonists. Blacks—first brought to America from Africa as indentured servants shortly after the colony of Virginia was established—also were deemed inferior humans, especially after slavery was legalized in Virginia in the mid–1660s. For roughly a century and a half thereafter, blacks were brought from Africa en masse to do most of the hard labor in tobacco and cotton fields, and elsewhere. The physical care of slaves and their children was considered to be the responsibility of the slaveholders. But needy free blacks also were neglected by the American social welfare system. They were left to care for themselves, which they sometimes did through the formation of covert mutual benefit societies. Years after the colonial period, other minority groups, such as Mexican and Chinese immigrants, were similarly overlooked.

Benjamin Franklin

The role Benjamin Franklin played in the history of government entitlement programs was a minor part of the Pennsylvanian's vast legacy. Franklin is far better known for many of his other accomplishments. In fact, even for a man who died at the age of eighty-four, he seemed to have lived several lives at once.

Born in Boston in 1706, Franklin was one of seventeen children, only eleven of whom lived to adulthood. His career as a writer began at the age of fifteen, when he submitted his first letters to a newspaper, the *New England Courant*, which was run by an older brother. Franklin knew that, brother or no brother, his work would never be published because of his age, so he invented a woman he called "Silence Dogood" and sent in the letters in her name. The letters became a popular feature in the newspaper, but trouble resulted when Franklin's brother found out the writer's identity.

Franklin moved to Philadelphia in 1723 to get away from family troubles. He found work there as a printer and later was able to open a print shop of his own. That business was so successful that in 1729 he bought and began to publish the popular *Pennsylvania Gazette* newspaper. He often wrote for the paper himself. It was from this base that Franklin's career really took off.

Poor Richard's Almanac, which Franklin began publishing in 1733, was for almost thirty years one of the most popular annual books in colonial America. An almanac is a book containing weather predictions, tables for high and low tides, and other information useful to farmers and fishers. *Poor Richard's* was doubly popular because it also contained Franklin's own writing, always under pen names. "A penny saved is a penny earned" is one of many famous sayings that originated with Franklin and his almanac.

In his forties, Franklin became an inventor. His many inventions include the lightning rod, a metal pole mounted on top of a building, to carry the electrical charge of lightning strikes into the ground, thus preventing the building from catching fire.

Later in life Franklin became involved in politics, becoming a colonial representative to the English Parliament. He was part of a team of five that helped write the Declaration of Independence in 1776, and he also was one of its signers. He was America's first ambassador to France and was later elected a representative to the Constitutional Convention, making him one of only six men to have signed both the U.S. Constitution and the Declaration of Independence. Franklin died in Philadelphia in 1790.

Government Entitlements

Meanwhile, the number of needy people in colonial America continued to grow. Several factors contributed to this growth, including two deadly battles. The French and Indian War (1754–1763) and the Revolutionary War (1775–1783) killed thousands of people and disabled thousands more. Also left to fend for themselves were large numbers of unskilled widows and orphans, who often ended up seeking public assistance because they could not find work. Other factors contributing to the rising number of needy people included the prevalence of infectious diseases such as scarlet fever, smallpox, and measles, and the population growth of major cities, including Boston, New York, and Philadelphia, where the number of jobs available failed to keep pace with the heavy streams of new arrivals looking for work.

The colonies' declaration of independence from England in 1776, and the subsequent formation of the United States of America, brought more population growth. America was to become a world power based on the ideals of democracy and opportunity. From the eighteenth century on, many people have come to the United States seeking those advantages. In 1790, the first year of the U.S. Census, there were fewer than 4 million people living in America. But just ten years later, that number had grown by 35 percent to 5.3 million. The population continued its rapid climb. By 1900, there were more than 76 million people living in the United States. Today, more than 300 million people call the United States their home.

The dramatic rise in population was not due solely to the great influx of immigrants. An across-the-board increase in Americans' life span—thanks in part to medical advancements and improved nutrition—contributed greatly to the country's population boost. In 1800 the average American died before the age of forty. By 1900, the average American was living to be almost fifty. The increase in average life expectancy, generally considered to be a good thing, negatively affected America's social health systems, however. This was primarily because of the increased number of older people, who often needed some form of assistance.

Industrialization affected America's social programs, as well. The invention of machines and the creation of factories caused America to shift from its agricultural roots to a manufacturing-based economy. This caused people to move away from rural areas into bigger cities where factory jobs could be found. This urbanization fractured families, though, for often only the father made the move. The women and children left behind required support—and again society was called upon to provide it.

The volatility of industrialized businesses also created new insecurities for American workers. When the economy was good, the so-called boom times, jobs and wages were plentiful, and the numbers of those requiring welfare declined as a result. But during bad, or "bust" times, the number of needy persons rose dramatically.

The casualties of the American Civil War—similar to the French and Indian and Revolutionary Wars before it—added more people to the list of needy. The Civil War spurred the creation of special laws intended to help wounded veterans, war widows, and orphans. Ordinary citizens also stepped up their charitable giving during this period.

After the war ended in 1865, America entered a period of prosperity and expansion the likes of which had never before been seen. In general, that meant more work for those seeking it. But there also were major social issues created by the end of the war. Most significantly, the victory of the anti-slavery North over the pro-slavery South resulted in the conclusive abolition of slavery in the United States. Millions of slaves were freed, yet most lacked the education and skills necessary to get jobs outside the farming industry. Thus many were not only unemployed but homeless, as well.

The federal government stepped in to help, creating an agency called the Freedmen's Bureau to provide relief to former slaves, and also to many dislocated white people. The bureau issued food

Government Entitlements

and clothing, helped locate family members, offered education, secured living arrangements, and much more. The bureau operated until 1872.

This period in U.S. history also was a time when society began to scrutinize the poor more closely than ever before. Charles Darwin's 1859 book, *On the Origin of Species*, played a large role in causing this scrutiny. The English naturalist theorized that living creatures had evolved throughout time and that the strongest of any given species prospered, while the weak ones were weeded

A teacher and her students stand in front of a Freedmen's School in North Carolina just after the Civil War.

Historical Overview

out by what Darwin dubbed natural selection. Darwin applied his theory to humans as well as to other living organisms.

Philosopher Herbert Spencer went one step further, applying the theory of national selection to economics, politics, and social issues. The result was Social Darwinism, whose adherents believed that the poor simply were weaker individuals, and therefore poverty was a natural occurrence that little could be done about. Social Darwinists placed the blame directly on the poor for their own circumstances in life and, from this position, proposed to justify shoddy ethical decisions that affected the treatment of less fortunate individuals. Many of the tenets of Social Darwinism exist today, including the belief that "only the strong will survive," which is the basis for many business models.

Created in response to Social Darwinism, charitable societies began to spring up in many cities across the United States during the latter half of the nineteenth century. The first was founded in 1877 in Buffalo, New York. The idea of these umbrella groups was to coordinate a municipality's numerous local charities and institute a more scientific system in which records were kept on each person who received assistance. The goal was to prevent duplication of benefits and also to eliminate the ambiguous rules on which so many groups based their assistance. The records also helped promote cooperation among givers. Either paid staff members or volunteers thoroughly investigated each applicant to determine the cause of his or her poverty. The societies then determined a course of action designed to address the individual's immediate issues and, more importantly, to form a foundation of self-sufficiency that would ideally prevent the development of any further problems.

At the same time, another method of helping the poor, known as the settlement movement, sprung up in numerous cities across the United States. A group of people—generally young women from relatively well-off families—would move to a poor area and live together in what was called a settlement house. The group

Charles Darwin

Charles Darwin was born in 1806 in England. At the age of twenty-five, he boarded the British ship *HMS Beagle* to participate in a scientific expedition to gather plant and animal samples. Darwin was not the only scientist to theorize that animals, including humans, evolved over time and shared distant ancestors; his contemporary, Alfred Russel Wallace, also theorized about evolution. However, the five-year voyage of the *Beagle*, the evidence Darwin collected during the trip, and the subsequent book, *On the Origin of Species*, marked the first major scientific work in the field, supported by data from animal and plant samples collected all over the world.

Darwin's theory, based on observations of the living creatures as well as on fossils he brought back to England, was that variations (also called "mutations") randomly occur in all species. When a mutation makes the individual who has it more able to adapt and survive, that individual will tend to pass the mutation along to its offspring. Over time, as more members of the species carry the new traits, a favorable mutation will become "normal" for that species.

Some mutations are obvious, such as the size difference between an African lion and a common house cat. These felines obviously share a common ancestor, but the lion's size and power allow it to survive as a hunter in the African plains, while the much smaller house cat is better suited for urban environments, including the homes of humans. In other cases, the advantages of certain mutations are not so obvious, such as color differences among different species of fish.

Darwin avoided commenting on the religious and social implications of his work, although many others did it for him. The theory that man and apes both evolved from a common ancestor contradicts the biblical story of creation, for example, and has thus been roundly criticized by fundamentalists ever since the publication of *On the Origin of Species.*

The philosophical stance that became known as Social Darwinism was first advanced in the 1830s, shortly after Darwin began presenting his research publicly to scientific groups. Social Darwinism held that such character traits as intelligence, work ethic, and morals could be passed on to offspring much like physical mutations, and so one could regard poor and indigent people as lower, less-evolved forms of life.

Darwin died in 1882 in England. He is buried in Westminster Abbey, London, near other famous Britons, including Isaac Newton, Charles Dickens, and Rudyard Kipling.

would work with individual community members and families to help them improve their lot in life. Oftentimes, such houses became community gathering places. One of the best-known settlement houses was Hull House in Chicago, which was cofounded in 1889 by a future Nobel Peace Prize winner named Jane Addams.

At the turn of the twentieth century, private social support efforts began to give way to public ones. The shift was inspired by people's desire to take care of needy children. In 1909 President Theodore Roosevelt called for the inaugural White House Conference on the Care of Dependent Children. The conference helped establish new national policies on the care of youth. Rather than placing dependent children in orphanages or institutions, as had been the usual practice up to this point, the new focus was on keeping minors in the family home at all costs. To this end, widows and single mothers were given pensions that would help the families to stay together, with support for the children. The conference also helped establish the federal Children's Bureau and the Foster Care Program. Similar conferences were held in subsequent years to help establish standards in the areas of humanitarian concern such as child labor and health care.

The Progressive Era

Social reform movements came during what was called the Progressive Era, which began in the late 1800s and lasted through the 1920s. Progressivism had developed in response to the many problems created by industrialization. Improvements in labor laws, including those applying to children, were on the Progressive agenda, as were government corruption, unethical business practices, and other economic, moral, political, and social issues. Laws enacted during this period dramatically changed the role of government and led to many restructuring efforts related to social welfare. Key legislation passed during this time included Amendments Sixteen through Twenty to the U.S. Constitution, which respectively created

Jane Addams

American's settlement house movement may have Jane Addams's fingerprints all over it, but it is by no means the only social reform work she spearheaded. Addams was born in 1860 in Cedarville, Illinois, to a prosperous family, and from an early age suffered from health problems that would remain with her for the rest of her life. She was born with Pott disease, tuberculosis of the spine. Addams's father, John, was well known throughout the region. He owned a local grain mill, served sixteen years as an Illinois senator, fought as an officer in the Civil War, and was a friend of Abraham Lincoln.

Jane Addams was an excellent student and graduated at the top of her class in 1881 from Rockford Female Seminary. When Addams was twenty-seven she took a trip to Europe with a friend named Ellen Starr. While the young women were touring London they visited Toynbee Hall, a settlement house dedicated to helping underprivileged boys. Inspired by what they saw, Addams and Starr returned to the United States and in 1889 opened Hull House, a similar community center for poor residents of Chicago. The community house became a huge success, eventually providing food, shelter, and education to approximately two thousand people per week. Other communities soon established settlement houses of their own.

Addams also was an early leader for the women's rights movement. She believed women should have a say in government decisions and therefore should be able to vote, a right that did not come to all American women until 1920. In her later years, Addams spoke out against U.S. involvement in World War I and was harshly criticized in the media. Undeterred, she continued her efforts to push for peaceful resolutions to conflicts. In 1931 Addams became the first American woman, and the second woman ever, to win the Nobel Peace Prize, which she shared with Nicholas Murray Butler, the founder of the Carnegie Endowment for International Peace. In 1935, after several years of failing health, Addams died at the age of seventy-four.

Historical Overview

an income tax, allowed citizens to directly elect their senators, banned the sale of alcohol, and guaranteed women the right to vote. The Progressive movement was a strong one, but it lost considerable momentum in the first decade of the twentieth century, when the U.S. government shifted much of its attention toward World War I, which had broken out in Europe in 1914.

A period of prosperity began in 1918, with the end of World War I, and social reform was not a priority. The economy grew, technological innovations were abundant, and many Americans became rich from investing in the stock market. But when the market crashed on what became known as Black Tuesday—October 29, 1929—all that changed. Collectively, wealthy investors lost billions of dollars overnight. Banks failed, and businesses shuttered their doors. Within three years, roughly one out of every four Americans was unemployed. It was obvious that change was necessary.

The presidential election of 1932 brought that change to America. That was the year the Democratic governor of New York, Franklin Delano Roosevelt, won the U.S. presidency in a landslide over the Republican incumbent, Herbert Hoover. Roosevelt believed the Depression stemmed from fundamental flaws in the economy and that government intervention was needed. When he took office in early 1933, Roosevelt embarked aggressively on that corrective path with a series of steps collectively known as the New Deal.

In years past, the federal government had taken a backseat to local and state governments, as well as private entities, in dealing with social welfare issues. This state of affairs was to cease. The social welfare system of the United States was greatly expanded, and many new programs were created. Almost immediately Roosevelt's administration created the Federal Emergency Relief Administration, which was in charge of providing money to states to help struggling individuals and families. Emergency relief programs, banking reform laws, and work-relief programs were quickly

Government Entitlements

passed. Some of the reforms implemented by the New Deal are still around. Most prominent among them is the Social Security Act, which created a solution to the problem of old-age pensions.

President Roosevelt believed every American citizen should have a certain level of economic security. Many Americans agreed, but there were many others who did not and who argued against Roosevelt's reforms.

Positive effects of New Deal policies began to appear as the 1930s drew to a close, heralding the end of the Great Depression. But by 1940, the year after the start of World War II, many new military-related jobs and entrepreneurial opportunities boosted the American economy even further. That prosperity continued after the war ended in 1945 and carried through much of the 1950s. During this time, federal legislation on issues related to social welfare was rare.

Still, many families were struggling to make ends meet. The federal government was well aware of the issue, and shortly after he was elected president in 1964, Lyndon B. Johnson—who had become president after the assassination of his predecessor, John F. Kennedy, whom he served as vice president—declared a War on Poverty in the United States. His chosen weapon was the Economic Opportunity Act, which was drafted in February and signed into law in August. At the signing, Johnson said:

> For so long as man has lived on this earth poverty has been his curse. On every continent in every age men have sought escape from poverty's oppression. Today for the first time in all the history of the human race, a great nation is able to make and is willing to make a commitment to eradicate poverty among its people. . . . For the million young men and women who are out of school and who are out of work, this program will permit us to take them off the streets, put them into

Historical Overview

President Lyndon Baines Johnson created government job-training programs as part of his War on Poverty. Here, Johnson talks to workers at one such program center in Philadelphia.

work training programs, to prepare them for productive lives, not wasted lives. In this same sound, sensible, and responsible way we will reach into all the pockets of poverty and help our people find their footing for a long climb toward a better way of life. We will work with them through our communities all over the country to develop comprehensive community action programs—with remedial education, with job training, with retraining, with health and employment counseling, with neighborhood improvement. We will strike at poverty's roots.

Government Entitlements

The Economic Opportunity Act established the Office of Economic Opportunity, which created and directed educational, training, and work programs across the country. Many of the programs designed to help fight the War on Poverty were phased out by future administrations, and Congress repealed the act itself in 1981, the first year of Ronald Reagan's presidency. However, some of the strongest programs established by Johnson's act are still with us: food stamps, Medicare, Medicaid, and Head Start, a national program that helps educate, provide health care for, and feed low-income, preschool-age children.

Whether owing to Johnson's efforts, or to other economic factors, the early years of the War on Poverty saw measurable improvements. By 1974, the national poverty rate was nearly chopped in half from its 1960 level: from 22 percent down to 11.2 percent. Communities also became more involved in decisions that directly affected them. That did not mean Johnson's war was without critics. Critics believed the help given by the Economic Opportunity Act created a system in which many recipients became reliant on government aid, falling into a cycle of dependency. Opponents of the president's policy argued that the antipoverty programs created a culture in which people felt entitled to help from the government.

During his 1992 presidential campaign, Democrat Bill Clinton vowed to "end welfare as we know it," by placing strict limits on how long a person can be on welfare before having to find a job. It was not until August 1996, however, that President Clinton was able to sign into law the Personal Responsibility and Work Opportunity Reconciliation Act (also known as the Welfare Reform Act). The act ended the Aid to Families with Dependent Children (AFDC) program that had been created as part of the New Deal, and replaced it with Temporary Assistance for Needy Families (TANF). The new program shifted many of the responsibilities for administering welfare programs back to the states, required re-

Historical Overview

cipients to go to work within two years of receiving assistance, and placed a lifetime limit on welfare of five years, although there were some minor exceptions to the rules.

Statistically, TANF was highly successful. The number of families receiving welfare dropped significantly, and many former recipients found work. However, as the program's critics were quick to point out, many of the jobs found by former welfare recipients were low-paying, which basically left the new workers in the same dire financial situations that had led them to welfare. Going to work also added costs people had not had as welfare recipients, including the expenses of care for young children and transportation to and from work. In spite of its shortcomings, however, the basic architecture of TANF remains in place today.

Americans take Social Security insurance for granted now, but back in 1939, when benefits were new, this unemployed lumberjack had his new Social Security number tattooed on his arm.

2 Social Security

WHEN THE TERM SOCIAL SECURITY WAS INTRODUCED to mainstream America more than seventy-five years ago, its definition was much broader than it is today. Back then, the law enabling the Social Security program was described as follows in its preamble:

> An act to provide for the general welfare by establishing a system of Federal old-age benefits, and by enabling the several States to make more adequate provision for aged persons, blind persons, dependent and crippled children, maternal and child welfare, public health, and the administration of their unemployment compensation laws; to establish a Social Security Board; to raise revenue; and for other purposes.

For most people today, "social security" has a much more specific meaning. Nowadays, the term simply refers to one portion of the lengthy Social Security Act—the "system of Federal old-age benefits." That system's official title is Old Age, Survivors, and Disability Insurance (OASDI). Although Social Security's definition may be more specific than it was some three-quarters of a century ago, the entitlement program itself is anything but simple. Social Security still is complex, controversial, and constantly changing.

The research committee compiling the data to support the original Social Security Act of 1935 determined one fact early on:

there was a clear need for some form of old-age pension in the United States. The committee came to this conclusion:

> The worker, after years of productive effort, has earned the right to rest; his advanced age or invalidity renders him incapable of an effective part in productive enterprise; [and] his continuance at work prevents a younger man from filling his place and gaining occupational skill, experience, and promotion. . . . The effect of destitution and dependency is enormously expensive not only in the cost of actual assistance rendered by governments, private charity, and the generosity of relatives and friends but also in the psychological results of the loss of self-respect and the constant fear of insecurity.

The committee's research data showed that only slightly more than half the residents of Washington, D.C., over the age of sixty-five were living independently, while almost 50 percent were dependent upon others for their survival.

Prior to the adoption of the Social Security Act in 1935, several states already had enacted old-age pension plans, and many more had considered doing so. However, all previous plans and ideas were voided when the federal act created an insurance program that guaranteed retirees age sixty-five or older an income for the rest of their lives.

The way the Social Security program worked was fairly straightforward: the earnings of all working people in America were to be taxed in accordance with the Federal Insurance Contributions Act (FICA), and all employers also would be taxed. The initial tax rate was set at 2 percent—half to be paid by the worker, half by the employer. The money collected was then placed in the newly created Social Security Trust Fund and distributed in the form of monthly benefits to workers during their retirement.

Social Security

The old-age pension program was highly popular thanks in part to its self-sustaining nature. The amount someone received upon retirement was based on the person's earnings during working years. The higher the wage and the more years worked, the higher the individual's Social Security check would be. The amount on a person's first monthly check would be the amount received every month as long as he or she lived. Social Security is funded by a pay-as-you-go (also known as "pay-go" or "paygo") system, in which taxes paid by current workers pay for the benefits of current retirees.

To implement the system, every worker was issued a card bearing a unique Social Security number. A twenty-three-year-old businessman from New York, John David Sweeney Jr., was widely reported to have been the recipient of the first Social Security card, in November 1936. Today, many historians believe Sweeney actually was not the first. Ironically, Sweeney died of a heart attack in 1974 at age sixty-one, a few years too early to have received any payments from the program. However, his widow did receive payments until her death in 1982. Despite the confusion over who received the first Social Security card, the identity of the recipient of the first Social Security *number* is known for certain. That distinction went to Grace D. Owen of Concord, New Hampshire.

During the first three years of the Social Security program, payments were simple lump sums given to the worker upon retirement. This was because the program was too new and the worker had not worked long enough after the program had been implemented to earn monthly benefits for the rest of his life. According to the U.S. Social Security Administration, the first person to receive one of the lump sums was a man from Ohio who was paid just seventeen cents because he had worked only one day while the program was in effect.

In 1940, the first year monthly checks were issued, the average monthly benefit paid out to retired workers was $22.71. But several major changes to the Social Security program were

A History of Pensions

The idea of pensions for the old, the infirm, and their families and survivors has been around in America since the Revolutionary War. The first comprehensive program intended to provide for the disabled, retirees, and the families of veterans was the Civil War Pension program, which began in 1862. It provided for cash payments to soldiers who were injured in the war or had served a certain number of years and then retired, and the families of deceased veterans who had been wounded in war. In some cases this led to very young women marrying very old men to get benefits. According to the *Los Angeles Times*, the last surviving widow of a Civil War veteran died in 2004, at age ninety-seven. She had married her husband when he was eighty-one years old and she was twenty-one.

Social Security was passed in 1935 and began in 1936. This famous part of President Franklin D. Roosevelt's New Deal was intended to provide pensions for retirees and people who could not work because of disabilities. The program assigns each person an identifying number, and a card bearing that number is issued to that person. Since the inception of the program, the Social Security Administration has changed the appearance of Social Security cards dozens of times.

Changes in the design of Social Security cards have been relatively minor and gradual over the years, the largest single change coming in 1983, when a counterfeit-resistant version was introduced, printed on the same type of paper as banknotes and with special ink designs that could not easily be copied. A 1988 design revision added a pattern that could not be seen with the naked eye; if one of the new cards was photocopied, however, the word "VOID" appeared on the copies.

The "VOID" pattern was removed in 2004 and replaced with some of the same high-tech anticounterfeiting measures now used on government-issued paper money. By the end of 2009, more than 420 million Social Security cards and numbers had been issued. The first three numbers of each person's card represent the area of the country from which the application was made.

When President Franklin D. Roosevelt signed the Social Security Act into law he was surrounded by Cabinet members and key members of Congress. Many on the outside, however, were critical of the new act, seeing it as a form of socialism that would lead to the downfall of democracy.

Government Entitlements

implemented as early as 1939; they included adding benefits for the worker's spouse and minor children, and adding a survivor's benefit to be paid to the family of any working parent who died before retirement. Such benefits can be paid to the worker's widow or widower, his or her unmarried children under the age of eighteen (or nineteen if they are attending an elementary or secondary school full time), and even the worker's parents, if they meet certain dependency criteria.

Large financial adjustments were made to the Social Security system in 1950, after President Harry S. Truman called for an expansion of the 1935 act. That expansion granted benefits to about 10 million previously ineligible workers. A simultaneous cost-of-living adjustment (COLA) increased the amount of each recipient's monthly check to help keep up with inflation. The 1950 COLA was a whopping 77 percent. This helped push the amount a person could receive in Social Security benefits higher than the benefits for which they were eligible from the old-age assistance welfare programs many states had offered since the early 1900s. That first COLA made Social Security the more appealing option for many Americans. In 1949 old-age assistance welfare programs were paying recipients an average of $42 per month, while Social Security was only paying about $25. But, thanks to COLAs, by 1955 the average retired worker's monthly Social Security check had risen to almost $70. There followed increases for much smaller percentages at various points, into the early 1970s. Social Security payments rose accordingly. The average person's monthly check in 1970 was $123.82. By the end of that decade, that amount had more than doubled.

The payment increases in the middle to late 1970s were due to a 1972 amendment to the Social Security Act that created, beginning in 1975, automatic yearly COLAs. The 1975 amendment also established a program called Supplemental Security Income (SSI), which provided for payments to aged, blind, and disabled persons who had little or no income to pay for basic needs such

The First Check

Retired legal secretary Ida May Fuller was the first person ever to receive a monthly Social Security check. The check, in the amount of $22.54, was issued January 31, 1940.

Fuller was born in 1874 in Vermont, where she attended school with a future president of the United States, Calvin Coolidge. In 1905, after a brief stint as a teacher, she became a legal secretary. She lived in Vermont her entire life, never married, and never had children, but she—like the rest of the nation's workers—began paying into Social Security by way of payroll taxes in 1937. Payroll taxes are automatically deducted from a worker's pay, so that paychecks are not in the full amount of the person's salary.

Fuller filed her retirement claim at age sixty-five in November 1939, having paid Social Security taxes for about three years. She continued to receive her Social Security benefits until she died at the age of one hundred in 1975. Fuller paid a total of $24.75 in Social Security taxes and received $22,888.92 in Social Security benefits.

Government Entitlements

as food, clothing, and shelter. The SSI program differs from basic Social Security in two ways. First, it is federally funded by general taxes rather than by taxes collected for Social Security. Second, eligibility is in no way related to how long, if at all, a person worked prior to applying for benefits.

The Social Security Act has seen many other major changes, as well. Disability insurance (SSDI) was added in 1956, and this program was amended in 1960. The new insurance extended benefits to injured workers of all ages, as well as their dependents, and to children and adults who have been disabled since birth.

A 1961 amendment to the Social Security Act gave all male workers the option of retiring early, at age sixty-two, and allowed those who did so to still receive a reduced portion of their Social Security benefits. Women had been granted that early-retirement option five years earlier.

Medicare

Perhaps the most significant change ever made to the Social Security Act came from amendments signed into law by President Lyndon B. Johnson, on July 30, 1965. The amendments created two important programs: Medicare, which offers government-funded health insurance to persons sixty-five and over, and Medicaid, which offers a similar insurance for the poor. President Johnson, who believed Medicare to be a vital program for American society, observed: "Many of our older citizens are still defenseless against the heavy medical costs of severe illness." In a symbolic move, Johnson signed the Medicare amendment in the presence of Harry S. Truman. Years earlier, during his own presidency, Truman had pushed for the expansion of Social Security and the creation of a national health insurance program.

Medicare was a great help for many seniors, particularly because it brought them peace of mind as they dealt with the often unavoidable health problems associated with aging. Before Medicare existed, many older Americans had difficulty obtaining any form of insurance at all. Private providers would not insure them because they were statistically at a high risk of becoming ill. This meant that seniors who lacked insurance had to pay their medical expenses out of their own pockets, and those who suffered from a major and/or lengthy illness often wound up penniless. It was true, as well, that many uninsured seniors chose not to seek medical treatment for their illnesses because they feared the costs would exhaust what assets they had.

Medicare coverage has evolved over the years. Today, it is divided into two main parts. Part A is automatically available to most Americans over the age of sixty-five. It is paid for by payroll taxes collected from workers through the Social Security system. Part A is a hospital insurance program that addresses many services provided during inpatient care and at selected other facilities. Services include blood transfusions, hospice care, hospital stays, and nursing home costs. Medicare does not necessarily cover the total cost of these services. Often patients must pay a share out of their own pockets, or at least what is called a copayment: that is, a portion of the cost of the treatment. Copayments—which typically are quite small—generally must be made prior to receiving treatment.

Unlike Part A, Medicare's Part B is not a free service. Recipients have to pay monthly premiums, just like those who hold health insurance policies from the private sector. The premiums help cover the costs of the program and often are deducted directly from Social Security checks. Part B is a form of supplemental medical insurance that covers many of the services not covered by Part A: visits to doctors' offices, medical equipment, ambulance costs, some preventive services such as screening for certain diseases, and more. Medicare also offers a combination of the Part A and Part B programs, which often is referred to as Part C coverage or Medicare Advantage. There also is a Part D coverage, which contributes to the cost of prescription drugs.

Government Entitlements

From its inception, Medicare has had its share of opposition. Initially, that resistance came from none other than the American Medical Association, which did not want the government in any way involved in patient-doctor relationships. Many conservative politicians were opposed to Medicare, as well. Their main objection was that such a program would lead to socialism, a form of political organization in which the government controls key resources and assures that they are distributed equally to all.

Prominent conservative politicians of the day, such as Ronald Reagan and Barry Goldwater, spoke out publicly against Medicare. In the early 1960s, long before he entered national politics, Reagan said, "[I]f you don't [stop Medicare] and I don't do it, one of these days you and I are going to spend our sunset years telling our children and our children's children what it once was like in America when men were free." Goldwater, who ran for president against Lyndon Johnson in 1964, was particularly harsh in his criticism of Medicare and pessimistic about the direction in which he feared such a program might lead the country. He said, "Having given our pensioners their medical care in kind, why not food baskets, why not public housing accommodations, why not vacation resorts, why not a ration of cigarettes for those who smoke and of beer for those who drink?" But being conservative or liberal does not necessarily dictate where one stands on the issue of Medicare. For example, it was President George W. Bush, a conservative Republican, who signed Medicare's Part D into law in 2003.

Big Changes to Social Security Act

Adjustments made to the Social Security Act in 1977 helped financially stabilize the program by increasing payroll taxes and slightly lowering benefits for those who first became eligible to receive them in 1979. Financial problems with the program also were addressed by several major amendments made in 1983. Those amendments stemmed from changes suggested by the National Commission

Ronald Reagan

Ronald Reagan, the fortieth president of the United States, was elected in 1980 and again in 1984. He was a former Hollywood movie actor who had served as president of a union, the Screen Actor's Guild, and had been governor of California from 1967 to 1975.

Once known as a liberal Democrat, Reagan joined the Republican Party in the early 1960s, becoming active in conservative politics to the point of serving as spokesman for a campaign opposing the introduction of the Medicare program. In 1980, when Reagan was first elected president, the national economy was relatively stagnant, with high inflation and unemployment; he ran his campaign partly on a platform of restoring American prosperity by cutting taxes and limiting government spending.

As Reagan prepared to take office, America was experiencing its highest inflation since World War II: a rate of 12 percent. The inflation rate is a number representing the percentage by which prices rise in a given economy over a set period of time. To stimulate investment, Reagan cut the top-level income tax rates by more than two thirds, on the theory that wealthy people who had more money to spend would invest it in business expansion, thus creating more jobs and more economic prosperity for everyone. The more people were working and spending money, the more demand for goods and services would increase, thus allowing manufacturers and producers of services to keep price increases down, which in turn would lower inflation.

Reagan coupled his tax cuts with cuts in some government spending programs. Medicaid and the food stamp program experienced significant funding cuts during Reagan's two terms, and his administration also removed thousands of people from the Social Security disability rolls by challenging their disability claims.

Military spending increased sharply during Reagan's time in office, as did the national debt. Critics of the Reagan administration point to this president's massive expansion of the national debt, his slow response to the AIDS crisis, and numerous political scandals, including the so-called Iran-Contra scandal, a scheme in which some members of the national security apparatus allegedly sold weapons to Iran in order to funnel money to antigovernment rebels in Nicaragua, an activity Congress had banned. Ultimately, several high government officials and two military officers were convicted of crimes related to the scandal. The military officers' convictions were later vacated, and members of the Reagan administration were pardoned by another Republican president, George H. W. Bush.

Another major problem Reagan faced during his tenure was the collapse of the savings and loan industry, a financial services debacle that led to what was then the largest stock market crash since the Great Depression. Reagan's supporters, nevertheless, say that his aggressive tax cuts reinvigorated a stagnant American economy and that his staunch pro-America stance in world affairs led to the restoration of national pride. In either case, his presidency is remembered as one of the most significant ever in terms of shaping world events.

Social Security

When President Ronald Reagan took office in January 1981, one of his mandates was to privatize Social Security. The outcry from the public made that change impossible to implement.

on Social Security Reform, which was created by Ronald Reagan, who was then president. Reagan also signed the 1983 amendments into law. While doing so, he said, "This bill demonstrates for all time our nation's ironclad commitment to Social Security," and "Franklin Roosevelt's commitment that Social Security must always provide a secure and stable base so that older Americans may live in dignity." Reagan's stance on the issue of Social Security had completely flipped from his position some two decades earlier. Now, it appeared that Reagan believed that Social Security was a good thing, although he also suggested that workers who proved they had saved enough for retirement years be allowed to opt out of the government-backed program.

The main purpose of the 1983 amendments was to help shore up the system's finances so the program would be able to cover the retirement of the baby boom generation, the large group of Americans born between 1946 and 1964. Today, the first wave of baby boomers has just begun to retire. Owing to the sheer numbers of

Government Entitlements

baby boomers, in 2010 Social Security had to pay more out to retirees than it collected in taxes. From that point, Social Security has been drawing from its reserves and will continue to do so until they run out, which is projected to happen around the late 2030s. When that happens, it is estimated that tax income will be enough to pay recipients roughly 75 percent of their projected benefits through 2083. In 1983 Social Security's trust fund was scheduled to last until at least 2063. The actual estimated date is adjusted yearly, based on a complicated formula involving economic factors such as employment numbers and the overall health of the economy.

Medicare's current situation is almost as dire. That program's Hospital Insurance Trust Fund already pays out more in benefits than it takes in. Thus, trust fund assets are now being spent and are expected to be exhausted by 2017.

There are many reasons for Social Security's struggles. In addition to the huge number of people eligible for benefits is the lessening of the number of contributors to the program. In 1950 there were sixteen workers paying into Social Security for every person receiving benefits. By 2006, only slightly more than three people were paying in for each person receiving benefits. The ratio continues to shrink with every passing year. Unfavorable ratios of those paying in to those taking out place a huge strain on any pay-go system.

One reason for those unfavorable ratios is that people are simply living longer than they were when the program was implemented. When the Social Security Act was signed into law in 1935, the average life expectancy in the United States was sixty-two years. Thanks to advances in nutrition, medicine, and overall living conditions, American children born in 2010 may expect to live, on average, almost seventy-eight years.

High levels of unemployment also impact Social Security, since when there are fewer people working, there are fewer people paying into the system. Sometimes, when job prospects are low, people retire earlier than they had intended, which means that they begin collecting their Social Security checks well before they might normally have done.

Life on Social Security

Social Security was never intended to be anyone's sole means of income. When the program began, it was meant to supplement other retirement monies, such as those from work pensions and savings accounts. But many people today have neither pensions nor savings. Their monthly Social Security check is the only form of income they receive. Living on that money alone is not easy.

That is a fact Beverly Nash of Dallas, Texas, knows too well. In 2009, when she was seventy-four years old, Nash spoke to the *Dallas Morning News* about her struggles with Social Security as her only source of income. To survive on the $960 she received each month, she reported having to shop for clothes at secondhand stores, clip coupons, and keep her electrical bills down by using battery-powered lights around her house. Nash—who was born at the height of the Great Depression—told the interviewer, "I learned as a child how to hold onto a dollar, and I've never forgotten. 'If you can't afford it, you don't need it.' That's how I've survived."

Karen Raymond was sixty-six years old in 2007 when he spoke with a reporter about his Social Security woes. The rural Michigan man's monthly payment was only five dollars less than Nash's, but his situation was far worse than the Texas woman's. Raymond said he could never even consider renting a movie or going out to dinner. Nor could he afford to paint his house, whose appearance he called "disgusting." For roughly one in five Americans over the age of sixty-five, such as Raymond, Social Security is the only source of income. That adds up to more than 10 million people, many of whom neither made enough money during their working years to save for retirement or accumulate any real assets nor had jobs that afforded them pensions.

In January 2010, more than 52 million people received some

form of monthly Social Security benefit. The average amount was $1,066: less than $13,000 a year. By comparison, a person working full time for the federal minimum wage of $7.25 an hour made more than $15,000 a year, or an average of about $200 per month more than someone on Social Security. While that may not seem like a lot, it is approximately 20 percent more than the average Social Security recipient has. And most American workers make far more per hour than the federal minimum wage of $7.25.

Yet even though most people who have no income other than Social Security are receiving less than the minimum wage, there are some who take issue with the system's financial sustainability. Republican congressman Ron Paul of Texas believes the days of both Social Security and Medicare are numbered for financial reasons and that serious problems await each program not too far down the road. Paul says, "When it comes to Social Security and Medicare, the federal government simply won't be able to keep its promises in the future. That is the reality every American should get used to, despite the grand promises of Washington reformers. Our entitlement system can't be reformed—it's too late." Such sentiments are not original with Paul. They are the same arguments critics of the program have been offering for years.

Still others believe Social Security is nothing more than a Ponzi scheme—a system that pays old investors with the money of current investors, thus running the risk of not having enough new investors to cover obligations to existing clients.

Privatization

The future of Social Security is one of the most controversial issues facing America today. Exactly what should be done with the program—and also how to help all the people it currently supports and those who will require its support in the future—are the main concerns people have. Privatization is one solution that has been offered on and off for many years by Republicans.

Social Security

The basic idea behind privatization is that while people are still part of the workforce, they should be allowed to manage a portion, or all, of the amounts now deducted from their paychecks as FICA taxes. The theory is that people can make more money by investing on their own than they can by means of a government program that is expensive to administer. The theory goes that the heirs of savvy investors also stand to benefit more than they do with today's setup. Currently, when the person receiving Social Security—or the surviving spouse—dies, the benefits go away, as well. The rest of the surviving family gets nothing.

Private retirement accounts, on the other hand, may be passed on in accordance with the deceased person's wishes. Leftover monies that started out as payroll taxes do not revert back to the government. Australia, Germany, and Sweden are among the countries around the world that currently have privatized retirement systems.

Opponents of privatization, such as President Barack Obama, believe the risks associated with allowing individuals to manage their own retirement funds outweigh the potential benefits. What happens if people make poor decisions with their money? What if they invest in the stock market and it crashes right as they are about to retire, taking all their money down with it? How will the retirees manage then? Who will take care of them? With the current Social Security system, opponents of privatization argue, unlucky investors and heedless spenders alike are guaranteed some income regardless of market trends or poor personal decisions. Of course, for that guarantee to be valid, the government must figure out how to keep the program afloat financially. Some suggestions include raising the age of eligibility for the program, and gradually reducing the amount of promised benefits or slowing their growth.

Exactly what will happen to the Social Security program in the future remains a hotly debated topic, and one that undoubtedly will remain controversial for years and generations to come.

The widespread myth of the black welfare queen in her Cadillac was belied by the reality of statistics: the majority of people on welfare in 1963 looked like this family, whose many children were all eligible for the federal "Aid for Dependent Children" program.

3 Welfare

> It's just a social message, which you get all the time. People who know I'm on [welfare] will say, "Welfare's the worst thing that could have happened to black people...." It's a very humiliating experience. And the shame is really inside. I don't tell people I'm on aid now. You feel like you're living down to people's expectations and you're a statistic.... Most people just feel that you're not carrying your load in society. You know, that you're getting away with something. That everybody's taking care of you.

There are certain myths about welfare recipients, writes Jill Duerr Berrick in her book *Faces of Poverty*. Among them that the benefit payments they receive are too high and afford them a life of luxury. That most recipients are black women who keep having kids to increase the size of their checks. That the recipients are lazy. Berrick, a professor at the University of California, Berkeley, spent a year documenting the stories of five welfare recipients—including a single black mother named Darlene, who is quoted in the extract above—and offered evidence in her book to debunk each of those myths and many others. Welfare is likely the most controversial of all U.S. government entitlement programs. As Berrick suggests, those who receive welfare are subject to stereotype by the general public and politicians alike. As evidence, she cites the words of former California governor Pete Wilson, who

Government Entitlements

in the early 1990s proposed cutting welfare benefits in his state by 25 percent. He said doing so would simply mean that recipients "would have less for a six-pack of beer."

Welfare's Early Days

Like many other social programs, welfare's modern roots begin with the Social Security Act of 1935, which created Aid to Dependent Children (ADC). The program paid monthly lump sums directly to the mothers of children who were deemed needy, with the understanding that the funds were specifically for the children. The women were not supposed to spend the money on themselves, even though many were widows or single mothers and could not work because they had to take care of their kids.

Besides, for women with children, work was hardly an option and was even frowned upon by much of 1930s society. Moreover, women who did find jobs often were penalized by losing the ADC benefits they had been receiving for their children. Welfare caseworkers closely scrutinized each situation.

Initial welfare benefits were minimal. The monthly payout was $18 for the first child and $12 for each additional child. To be eligible, children had to be under the age of sixteen. The federal government covered one-third of the cost of each child: $6 for the first child and $4 for each additional child. Individual states were responsible for the rest.

From the beginning, welfare was meant to be a temporary solution or a supplement, like Social Security, and the low payments were indicative of that intent. The program was described as a defensive measure "designed to release from the wage-earning role the person whose natural function is to give her children the physical and affectionate guardianship necessary not alone to keep them from falling into social misfortune. . . ." That social misfortune was near for many children at the time. By mid–1938, roughly 604,000 children were receiving ADC payments.

Despite the seemingly large numbers, ADC remained a relatively minor social program throughout the 1940s and into the 1950s, when the numbers of recipients began to noticeably expand. Demographic shifts in the United States played a large role in this expansion. So did changes to the program itself, which loosened the qualification requirement. No longer did the program primarily serve dependent children and orphans, but now certain destitute women were eligible to receive benefits, as well. In 1962 the program changed its name to reflect this new philosophy. Thus, Aid to Dependent Children was renamed Aid to *Families* with Dependent Children (AFDC). Under this new moniker, the program's caseloads continued to grow rapidly.

Several more changes to the welfare program occurred during the 1960s, again partly for demographic reasons. As divorce rates increased across the country, so did the numbers of single-parent households in need of financial help. The number of children born out of wedlock also blossomed, especially among urban blacks. These circumstances were highlighted in a controversial report issued in 1965, titled "The Negro Family: The Case for National Action." The detailed report was written by Daniel P. Moynihan, who at the time was an assistant secretary for labor in President Lyndon Johnson's administration. The study, which commonly became known as the Moynihan Report, helped shape President Johnson's War on Poverty. It concluded that the breakdown of the traditional family structure played a major role in the rise of urban poverty.

Women also began to enter the workforce in greater numbers during this period. Black women, who had frequently been denied benefits based on loose and potentially bigoted definitions of what individual caseworkers thought constituted a "suitable home," now became eligible for help thanks to the civil rights movement and groups it helped create. For example, the National Welfare Rights Organization started suing persons in charge of dispensing benefits and, as a result, eligibility criteria were modified.

Those demographic changes led to a shift in public opinion of welfare in general. A majority of Americans had no problem with the original intent of the program, which was to assist needy children. But as more able-bodied women began receiving benefits, the general public began asking questions. Why should taxpayers subsidize these adults whose bad personal decisions had put them in a position of need? Author Berrick describes the shift thus: "In only a couple of decades, women on welfare were transformed from the 'deserving poor' into the 'undeserving poor.' To the American mind, welfare became synonymous with morally questionable behavior."

Food Stamps

Hunger was one of the main problems faced by those living on welfare. Although various food-supplementation programs had been on the books for decades—including an early food stamp program that ran between 1939 and 1943—it was not until the early 1960s that preventing hunger became a primary focus of the government. The boldest move on that front was the passage of the Food Stamp Act by Congress. A temporary food stamp program had been reenacted in 1961 under President John F. Kennedy, who was assassinated in 1963. His successor, Lyndon B. Johnson, asked Congress to make the program permanent, and it became one of the keystones of the new president's goal of expanding social welfare to achieve what he called the "Great Society."

The Food Stamp Act allowed low-income families the option of buying food coupons at a discount. Those coupons, or food stamps, could then be presented in grocery stores in exchange for any "food or food product for human consumption except alcoholic beverages, tobacco, those foods which are identified on the package as being imported, and meat and meat products which are imported." This legal definition clearly excluded many necessary goods people customarily buy in grocery stores, such as toothpaste and disposable diapers. Food stamps were made available to those

Welfare

This housewife was a beneficiary of the early food stamp program, which ran from 1939 until 1943.

who were on welfare, and other poor individuals also were eligible to apply. Individual states were responsible for determining who was eligible and the amount of stamps those who met the requirements could purchase.

The new program was a marked improvement over the haphazard food-subsidy programs that had come before it, although it was not without flaws. Despite their discounted price, the coupons still were too expensive for many families, making them useless to part of the population they were intended to serve. For this and other reasons, the food stamp program has been modified many times over the years. In 1977 food stamp recipients were no longer required to pay for the coupons. Later, the paper coupons were replaced by electronic cards, which are scanned at stores just like credit and debit cards. That switch has taken away some of the shame once associated with using food stamps, since it is much easier to prevent fellow customers from identifying the type of card one swipes than it was to hide the use of paper coupons.

In addition to introducing electronic cards that make the use of food stamp funds more discreet, officials in charge of the program have beefed up measures to prevent fraud. Over the years, food stamp recipients had been known to trade or sell their coupons for cash, which allowed them to buy nonfood items at will. The electronic cards, however, require the use of a personal identification number (PIN).

Medicaid

Sheri Stapler of Eugene, Oregon, is the mother of three young boys and is in her late-thirties. When she was seventeen weeks pregnant with her second child, Aidan, a doctor's examination discovered that the unborn baby had spina bifida—a birth defect in which the spinal canal and backbone do not close before birth as they should—and hydrocephalus, a buildup of spinal fluid inside the brain. Aidan's health problems required him to have surgery just three hours after he was born in October 2002, and he has had several additional surgeries. Later, doctors discovered that Aidan had a heart defect, and he recently was diagnosed with autism. Four times a day, his mother has to use a catheter to drain her son's bladder.

Stapler's husband, Randy, is a tow-truck driver who has held the same job for six years. His employer does not offer health insurance, and Aidan's medical bills are numerous. Fortunately, Stapler says, there is a government program available to help her out.

"Our family is just below the poverty line and can't always afford the best of the best for him," Stapler says. "Medicaid for us

Evolution of Food Stamps

During the Great Depression, the government's efforts to help farmers by paying them to grow certain crops resulted in surpluses. That is, more of some foods were grown than could be sold at market. Under the first food stamp program, created in 1939, a family receiving public assistance such as Social Security or welfare could use the benefits to buy orange stamps that could be redeemed for any food they chose. In addition, every dollar's worth of orange stamps was accompanied by fifty cents worth of blue stamps, which were redeemable only for foods that were on the surplus list.

So the program allowed a family that ordinarily spent $50 on regular groceries to also get $25 worth of whatever the government had too much of at the time—usually lower-priced items like beans and peas, but sometimes fresh fruit and dairy products such as butter.

The initial food stamp program was canceled in 1943 at the height of World War II, since "surplus" foods were now needed to feed those people assisting in the war effort. In addition, far fewer families were on public assistance thanks to the wartime hiring boom and the portions of salaries sent home by members of the military.

When the food stamp program was restarted in 1961, much as before, recipients got the "stamps" in paper books, with a money denomination printed on each stamp. The stamps were torn from the book to pay for groceries, and the grocer turned the stamps in to the federal government. The grocer then received from the government the total dollar amount on each batch of stamps submitted. Unlike the first program, there was no separate set of stamps for "surplus" foods; recipients simply used the stamps like money. As there were no food stamp denominations below $1, users received regular coins as change.

In the 1980s, a number of cutbacks and changes to the program were initiated, the most important being the introduction of electronic benefit transfer cards (EBTs). The EBT card, which is used just like a debit card to pay for groceries, reduces expenses by eliminating the need for grocers and government officials to keep track of paper stamps. It also allows grocers to be reimbursed faster, since they receive direct electronic transfers to their bank accounts, instead of waiting for a batch of stamps to be processed and a check to be issued. Different states implement the food stamp program in different ways, so the appearance of the cards varies from state to state; however, all states now use EBTs instead of paper.

is a lifeline. Without Medicaid, I don't think we would be able to see the doctors we need to see. Aidan would not have as many opportunities to have a normal life."

Just as Medicare provides medical coverage to those receiving Social Security, Medicaid covers low-income and disabled people. Both health care programs are overseen by the Centers for Medicare and Medicaid Services (CMS) of the U.S. Department of Health and Human Services, although Medicaid is administered by agencies in individual states, whereas Medicare is administered federally.

Medicaid was established in 1965 as part of the legislation that created Medicare: that is, in the same set of amendments to the original Social Security Act. Included among those initially eligible to receive Medicaid were low-income children lacking parental support, as well as their caretaker relatives, and the elderly, the blind, and individuals with disabilities. Roughly 8 million people initially were eligible for Medicaid, based on specific requirements. Those requirements were broken up into three categories: the categorically needy, the medically needy, and special groups. Examples of some of those who *may* be eligible in each group, as defined by the CMS, include the following:

Categorically Needy

- Families who qualify for the Temporary Assistance for Needy Families (TANF) program
- Pregnant women with children under six years old and a family income at or below 133 percent of the federal poverty level. For a family of three, the federal poverty level in 2009–2010 was $18,310 a year
- Children ages six to nineteen whose family income is up to 100 percent of the federal poverty level
- Caretakers of children under age eighteen (nineteen if still in high school)

Government Entitlements

Medically Needy
- Children under a certain age who are full-time students. The age varies from state to state
- Persons age sixty-five and older
- Blind persons
- Disabled persons

Special Groups
- Medicare recipients with limited income and financial resources
- Certain disabled workers
- Persons with certain medical conditions, such as tuberculosis and cervical cancer
- Individuals institutionalized with long-term care

Specific services available to those who qualify for Medicaid differ from group to group. Those who qualify as categorically needy, for example, receive help with inpatient and outpatient hospital services, laboratory procedures and X rays, medical and surgical help, and dental services, to name just a few areas of assistance.

Like all government entitlement programs, Medicaid has its problems. One of them is financial. As the Medicaid program has grown, and more people became eligible to receive benefits, costs went up, too, drawing increased scrutiny from both the general public and politicians. But, according to at least one study, those costs were not due solely to an increase in the number of Medicaid recipients. Inflated charges for medical services, manipulation of the system by individual states to increase their own federal payments, and fraud also have played large roles in the increased costs of Medicaid. Over the years, attempts have been made to rein in those costs. For example, President Barack Obama's health care reform bill—which was passed into law in 2010—containted several cost-cutting measures.

Welfare

The Welfare Reform Act of 1996 ended the longstanding Aid to Families with Dependent Children program and replaced it with Temporary Assistance for Needy Families. This change had a huge impact on Medicaid and other programs. No longer were those receiving welfare benefits automatically eligible for Medicaid. Many Medicaid benefits also were dropped, and legal immigrants entering the United States after August 22, 1996, became ineligible to receive Medicaid until they had been in the country for at least five years.

The switch from AFDC to TANF brought about by President Bill Clinton's welfare reform was motivated by several factors, including changes in society as a whole. For example, as women began to enter the workforce in greater numbers, the awareness that it was possible for women to stay home to raise their children, and receive payments to do so, generated resentments among some. For this and other reasons, it became increasingly obvious that changes to the welfare system were necessary, and TANF was the result. Foremost, while AFDC had been an entitlement program that guaranteed benefits to those who met certain criteria, TANF is not an entitlement program. It is a federal block grant program, in which states set their own eligibility guidelines. Some TANF regulations are as follows:

- Recipients must work as soon as they are determined to be ready to do so, or no later than two years after first receiving benefits.
- Recipients must participate in work activities—such as on-the-job training or work-related education—for a set number of hours each week.
- There is a five-year lifetime limit on the receipt of benefits, although states can exercise leniency in certain situations.

The number of people receiving cash benefits has declined significantly under TANF, prompting many to label it a success.

Government Entitlements

Child Support Enforcement

The makeup of the average American family has changed dramatically since 1950, the year the federal government first became deeply involved in the area of child support. At that time, only a small percentage of children were being raised in single-parent households. The stereotypical family structure—that of the father going to work, while the mother tended to the house and children, as portrayed in popular TV shows of the day like *Leave It to Beaver*—still was very much the standard. That is no longer the case. In the 1970s alone, the number of single-parent families increased at an annual rate of 8.9 percent and, although the rate of growth has slowed in recent years, the percentage has continued to climb. At the beginning of the twenty-first century, nearly 30 percent of all American families were led by just one person. A majority of those families were headed by women, who frequently were responsible for both parental roles.

The role of the government has increased accordingly. In 1975 the Federal Office of Child Support Enforcement was created to provide monies to states to establish their own Offices of Support Enforcement. The programs have expanded over the years and today offer help locating absent parents, establishing paternity, creating support orders that determine how much the absent parent should pay to take care of the children, and collecting that support money. In 2002 some $20 billion was collected from absent parents and distributed to the custodial parents. However, billions of dollars owed in child support also go uncollected each year, mainly because the absent parent cannot be found.

Child support is most frequently paid monthly by the noncustodial parent to the parent with whom the child, or children, lives. The support payments are typically required until the child is no longer a minor.

The federal government also finances the separate but closely related Child Care and Development Fund (CCDF), which helps

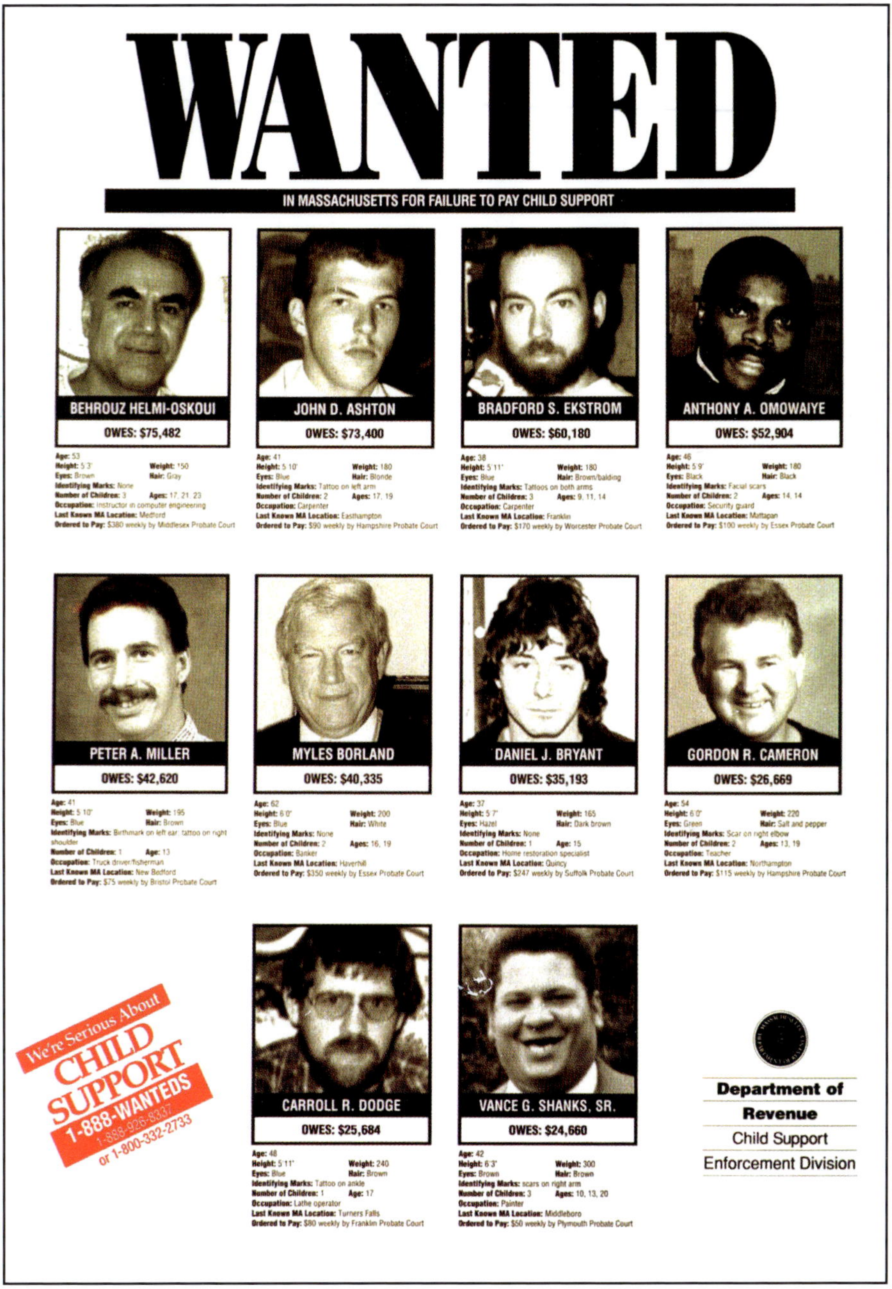

Welfare

This "Ten Most Wanted" poster doesn't show criminals as we normally think of them, but fathers who owe money for child support.

65

Government Entitlements

low-income families cover the cost of child care while the custodial parent works or goes to school. Like welfare, that program is administered by individual states.

WIC

The Special Supplemental Nutrition Program for Women, Infants and Children (WIC) provides nutritional assistance to low-income pregnant women, new mothers, and children up to the age of five. The goal is to provide healthy food options to those who qualify. Thus, WIC recipients receive supplemental foods that are deemed to be nutritious, and the women are instructed about what constitutes healthy eating.

WIC participants receive monthly checks, vouchers, or a benefit card that can be used to purchase healthy foods at grocery stores. Such foods include certain cereals and juices, eggs, milk, cheese, peanut butter, canned beans, and canned fish. WIC is not an entitlement program in the most basic definition of the term, which is that everyone who is eligible can apply for and receive assistance, regardless of the price tag associated with providing it. Instead, WIC is a federal block grant program that sets aside a specific amount of funding each year, although those who qualify for welfare or Medicaid also automatically qualify to receive WIC. In 2009 roughly 9.3 million Americans received WIC benefits each month. In 2010 the federal government appropriated more than $7 billion for the program.

Welfare Critics

Criticism of America's current welfare system—a generic term commonly used as a synonym for Aid to Families with Dependent Children and Temporary Assistance for Needy Families—comes from a variety of sources. Many of the critics cite the same issues Benjamin Franklin listed in his day: that giving benefits to individuals creates laziness and a dependency on charity that is difficult to overcome.

Welfare

Even some of those who have directly benefited from welfare programs now criticize them. Conservative author and philanthropist Star Parker is one such person. Parker lived on welfare for more than three and a half years in the 1980s, during which time she often abused the system. In 1995—years after she had left welfare and become a successful entrepreneur—Parker spoke on the *Oprah Winfrey Show* about her life on welfare. In her book *Pimps, Whores and Welfare Brats: From Welfare Cheat to Conservative Messenger*, Parker describes her experience and summarizes her appearance on the famous talk show as follows:

> I looked both of these women [current welfare recipients] in the eye and told them it was unfair for them to be at home raising their kids with taxpayers' dollars while the rest of us were putting our children in day care so we could work to support them. . . . The crowd let out a gasp when I told them about the nice one-bedroom apartment I could afford on my monthly $465 welfare check and how I earned extra cash selling [her state-issued health care stickers] on the black market to friends and acquaintances instead of using them for myself. I explained that not everyone was doing this, but welfare, by its very nature, discouraged finding a job and fostered a take-what-you-can-get attitude. To me it was no longer getting some government money to tide me over in hard times. I believed I was owed that bimonthly check, and by golly, I was gonna get what belonged to me!

The number of people receiving welfare benefits varies from day to day and from month to month. In 2009 the average number of people on welfare each month was slightly more than 4 million. The exact amount of each check depends on a variety of factors, such as how many children are in the household and the cost of living in the state the recipient lives in.

The Works Projects Administration created by President Franklin D. Roosevelt put millions of unemployed Americans to work and was instrumental in the creation of the infrastructure of dams, bridges, and roads that we still use today.

4 Unemployment Insurance

> For the past 4 years the American people have witnessed a tragic demonstration of the breakdown of our older methods of dealing with men and women who are out of work through no fault of their own. The fundamental case for unemployment protection lies in the fact that under a democratic form of society we are forced to prevent any large scale starvation. Funds must be provided somehow. . . . It is practical sense to build a system which will gather the funds in good times and disburse them in bad times. This simple theory underlies all formal proposals for unemployment insurance, for unemployment reserves.

The need to provide some type of assistance to those who were out of work was obvious to Stanley King, the author of the above passage, which was published in the *American Labor Legislation Review* in 1933. Written at the height of the Great Depression, King's words pointed out what he and many others believed to be the growing need for the federal government to establish some type of program to help Americans who were without jobs and struggling to provide for their families: nearly 25 percent of the country's population.

Title III of the Social Security Act of 1935 was written with that goal in mind. It called for help, as its subtitle stated, in the

Government Entitlements

form of "Grants to States for Unemployment Compensation Administration." Simply put, Title III was written to help workers through tough times after they had lost their jobs as a result of circumstances beyond their personal control.

As groundbreaking as Title III was, the United States was nowhere near the first country to offer temporary benefits to its unemployed workers. The United States and several other countries had offered various forms of compensation to unemployed workers for years, even decades in some instances. The first country to adopt a mandatory national unemployment program was Great Britain, in 1911. Five years later, the United States began to consider a broad approach to unemployment, although serious congressional investigation was delayed until 1928. Debate continued until August 1935, when President Franklin D. Roosevelt signed the Social Security Act, which enabled a nationwide program of unemployment insurance. By that time, Australia, Canada, Germany, Italy, Switzerland, and many other countries already had in place programs similar to Great Britain's to help their involuntarily unemployed citizens.

The unemployment insurance portion of the Social Security Act was as timely a piece of legislation as there ever was. The United States was two years removed from the worst of the Great Depression: the time when national unemployment rates reached a whopping 25 percent. A contemporary leftist paper sets the scene:

> [T]he distress of the masses was so great that there were open manifestations of suffering even leading to outbreaks. The breadlines then were blocks long, skilled workers and white-collar men, even women, had to resort to these wretched slops in order to keep life in their bodies. Flop houses 'sheltered' a portion of the homeless unemployed at night, while thousands slept on the park benches, in hallways and doorsteps. "Hoovervilles" sprang up on the outskirts of cities, on water fronts and

Franklin Delano Roosevelt

Franklin Delano Roosevelt was the thirty-second president of the United States, first elected in 1932. He was the only president in history to be elected to four terms, also winning in 1936, 1940, and 1944. In 1951, six years after Roosevelt's death, the Constitution was amended to prevent presidents other than Roosevelt's successor from serving more than two terms.

Roosevelt was born in 1882 in Hyde Park, New York, a member of a wealthy family of Dutch Americans who had lived in the area for generations. He began to practice law in 1908, but two years later he sought and won a seat in the New York State Senate. In 1913 he abruptly resigned his legislative seat because President Woodrow Wilson had appointed him assistant secretary of the Navy. In 1920 Roosevelt ran for vice president, but he and Democratic presidential candidate James Cox were soundly defeated. Roosevelt then returned to his work as a lawyer.

At age thirty-nine, the future president was stricken with polio, an illness that crippled his legs and left him unable to walk without braces and canes for the rest of his life. Because there was a social stigma attached to physical disability in those days, Roosevelt's condition was carefully hidden from the public. He was always photographed in ways to make his wheelchair less obvious, and he often stood when making speeches, with locking leg braces to keep him upright.

His ascent to the presidency came about largely because the nation was gripped in the economic crisis of the Great Depression, which many people blamed on the preceding administration of Republican Herbert Hoover. By the end of Roosevelt's first three months in office, however, unemployment levels in America had reached record highs, and to restart the economy, Roosevelt inaugurated a campaign of social programs and government spending.

Roosevelt's New Deal included massive public works projects such as the building of highways and dams, as well as many other government jobs programs that employed people whose expertise ranged from history and science to the arts. The New Deal also encompassed social insurance programs like Social Security, which provided pensions for retirees and the disabled. Another important Depression-era innovation was the Federal Deposit Insurance Corporation, which protects people against bank failures by guaranteeing that even if a member bank runs out of money, depositors will be reimbursed up to a maximum amount. Today, that amount is $250,000 per depositor.

Many New Deal programs still are operating today, while others were canceled after the United States entered World War II in December 1941. The unremitting wartime stress worked against Roosevelt's ongoing polio condition, however, and he died of a stroke in April 1945. At that time, he had been engaged in the early stages of an organization of international cooperation, the United Nations. His widow, Eleanor, was one of the authors of the UN's Universal Declaration of Human Rights, which was adopted in 1948. The rights this document lists as universally belonging to human beings reflect many New Deal principles.

Unemployment Insurance

on vacant lots. In these miserable colonies of down-and-outs, not only single men, but families moved into shacks which they built of tin cans, stray boards, strips of rags, etc., picking their living out of the garbage cans. The newspapers reported children fainting in the schools from hunger. Hundreds of thousands of boys and girls, many of them under twenty, and in fact whole families, took to the highways, hopped freights, and wandered from place to place, sleeping where they could, eating in "jungles" [encampments of homeless people], driven by police from city to city, hounded from state to state in an aimless, hopeless quest for the jobs that did not exist.

By 1935, unemployment levels had dropped to 20 percent, but by no means had the economy fully recovered from the stock market crash that had sent it plummeting downward six years earlier. The Great Depression was still very much on, and very much affecting millions of people—in the United States and other countries, as well.

How It Works

Unemployment insurance is funded from a tax levied on payrolls and collected by employers. Eligibility is based on a worker's earnings history, the reason for the unemployment, and the worker's availability to accept a job should one arise. Nearly all hourly and salaried workers are eligible for unemployment benefits, although railroad workers are covered by a separate program, as are federal civilian employees. Self-employed workers are not eligible to receive unemployment benefits because the program is based on the relationship between an employer and employee, and self-employed workers, by definition, are their own boss.

Eligibility requirements for unemployment insurance vary from state to state. During most times, workers who voluntarily

The Great Depression

The Great Depression was an economic collapse in the United States that began in 1929. Stocks on the New York Stock Exchange lost nearly 80 percent of their value, and across the world there was unemployment, accompanied by poverty and hunger.

The date generally accepted as marking the start of the Depression is October 29, 1929, sometimes called "Black Tuesday," the first day of the worst stock market crash in American history. Stock prices fell almost 25 percent in just two days, and continued to decline for an entire month.

Chief among the many economic factors that led to the crash and started the Depression itself was a practice called speculation: the borrowing of money to buy stocks, which were then used as collateral for the loan just obtained.

Since stock values depend on many variables, and the market was essentially unregulated at the time, some sellers were able to inflate the prices of the stocks they were buying and thus qualify for larger and larger loans. When those stock prices fell and stayed down, as they did in 1929, the banks and financial companies that had advanced the money for the loans were left with the now-worthless stocks. In many cases this drop in value of bank assets led to panics, as depositors discovered that certain banks were strapped for cash because of bad stock loans. Depositors then withdrew the money in their accounts, making the cash shortage even worse. In many cases, banks simply went out of business without being able to return the money of depositors who had not been among the first at the withdrawal windows.

Because so much money had been lost, people were unable to buy goods and services they normally would have been happy to pay for. This led to severe cutbacks in production at factories and farms, since there was no one buying goods. Millions of American workers lost their jobs. In addition, the effects spread across the world, since the United States had forged economic ties and developed many overseas markets in Europe and elsewhere after World War I, which ended in 1918.

President Roosevelt began turning the crisis around when he took office in 1933 by creating huge public works projects to develop the nation's infrastructure while giving employment to many. Roosevelt's New Deal combined emergency measures like the jobs programs with far-reaching social and economic legislation.

Despite massive government spending and other efforts, the Depression persisted into the late 1930s, and some historians say it didn't really end until the demand for manufactured products was renewed with the outbreak of World War II.

When the Great Depression began in 1929, people had no social safety nets. Millions lived on the streets and relied on the charity of private soup kitchens such as this one in Chicago in order to have anything to eat.

Government Entitlements

leave their jobs cannot receive benefits in any state, nor can those who are not actively seeking employment or those who were fired for causes deemed reasonable and just. In the early days of unemployment insurance, there was a thirteen- to sixteen-week limit on benefits. The federal Extended Unemployment Compensation Act of 1970 permitted states to pay benefits to unemployed workers for periods longer than twenty-six weeks during times of high unemployment. In the troubled years of the early twenty-first century, that limit has been extended repeatedly. The exact amount an unemployed worker now receives varies from state to state. In California, as of January 2010, the minimum weekly amount was $40, while the maximum was $450.

To receive benefits, former jobholders must apply through local unemployment agencies, either online or in person. A decision is then made to grant or deny benefits; the amount to be paid each week and in total is based on the guidelines for qualification of the state in which a person applies. Those who are denied benefits may appeal the decision.

The most obvious goal of unemployment insurance is to help make up for some of the income lost by people who no longer have jobs. But that is not the only goal. Indeed, unemployment insurance is also an economic stimulus measure. Providing unemployed workers with an income of any kind gives them the ability to continue to purchase goods and services, which in turn helps keep businesses—and those who operate them—employed.

The unemployment insurance program is not without its detractors. Some economic studies suggest that giving people money while they are unemployed discourages them from looking for a job, since in effect they are being paid *not* to work. Other studies have shown that "a large fraction of unemployed people suddenly started working again within a week or so of their benefit exhaustion date, despite having been without work for so many weeks prior: evidence that the benefits themselves were sustaining unemployment."

Unemployment Insurance: Good or Bad?

As is the case with many entitlement issues, high-ranking politicians often disagree on the validity of the unemployment insurance program. U.S. Senator Jon Kyl, a Republican from Arizona, said in March 2010 that unemployment insurance "doesn't create new jobs. In fact, if anything, continuing to pay people unemployment compensation is a disincentive for them to seek new work. . . . I'm sure most of [the unemployed] would like work and probably have tried to seek it, but you can't argue that it's a job enhancer. If anything, as I said, it's a disincentive." Other lawmakers, including Democratic Senator Max Baucus of Montana, disagree. According to Baucus,

> [Kyl] argues that unemployment insurance is a disincentive to jobs. Nothing could be further from the truth. I don't know anybody who's out of work and is receiving some unemployment insurance [who] believes that that payment is sufficient not to find a job. The payments are so much lower than any salary or wage would be, it's just ridiculous. I might add, there are five unemployed Americans today for every job opening in the economy. People are looking for work. They're not unemployed because of choice.

At least one study says that during normal times most people find a job or are recalled to work within the first several weeks of their unemployment period. But the same study showed that the chances of a person finding a job triple when the time remaining for receipt of unemployment benefits drops from six weeks to one week. The author of the study, economist Bruce D. Meyer, concludes, "If workers are bound to firms by implicit contracts, moving costs, specific human capital [education, experience, skills, etc.], or other reasons, firms have an incentive to base recall decisions on the length of UI [unemployment insurance] benefits."

Unemployment Insurance

By 2010, two years after the Great Recession had started, well over 9 percent of Americans found themselves out of work, and had run out of their unemployment benefits. Job fairs such as this one in McLean, Virginia, were mobbed.

Like all data about ongoing programs, the number of people receiving unemployment benefits—and the amount they receive—varies from week to week and year to year. In 2009, a period of atypically high unemployment across the country, some 12 million Americans received some form of unemployment benefit. Those payments came at a cost of nearly $103 billion.

The issue of unemployment insurance vaulted back into the national headlines at the end of 2007, when the United States entered an economic recession primarily caused by problems originating in the housing sector. The recession led to massive layoffs in a wide range of industries, especially those related to real estate, such as construction. Unemployment rates skyrocketed. In November 2007, the U.S. unemployment rate was 4.7 percent. By February 2010, that number had more than doubled, to 9.7 percent. Large

Government Entitlements

numbers of Americans were out of work, though the situation still paled in comparison to the days of the Great Depression.

Unemployment insurance is just one of the ways the United States helps its unemployed citizens. Other ways include the creation of programs intended to generate jobs, and general assistance programs: state and local measures that provide cash benefits to those who are not eligible for other types of help. General assistance is often the last resort for many needy people.

5 Workers' Compensation

A 23-year-old male was a blue-collar worker at a cinder block company in St. Louis, Missouri. He was cleaning a conveyor on May 8, 1930, when he lost his footing and fell into the heavy operating machinery. During the fall he severed his right arm above the brachial region and received a compound fracture of the left leg, as well as extensive rupturing of the muscles and nerve damage. . . . He also suffered extensive tearing of the perineum and rectum. . . . He was taken into emergency surgery. He sustained amputation of the right arm, permanent loss of the use of the right leg distal to the knee, lacerations and temporary muscle damage to the right lumbar region of the back and abdomen, atrophy distal to the left leg injury, and permanent partial loss of bowel function. . . . Unable to return to his former job, the injured worker . . . arranged to purchase eggs in bulk and sell them door-to-door. . . . He was awarded [by the Missouri Workers' Compensation Commission] $23.07 per week for a maximum of 400 weeks, or $6,152.00. . . . This patient survived in spite of the health care system of 1930, not because of it.

Government Entitlements

Centuries before the Social Security Act brought unemployment insurance and Social Security to the United States, programs were in place across the world to assist those who were injured on the job and therefore could not work. In fact, such laws were on the "books" shortly after the beginning of written history.

The laws of Ur, a city-state in ancient Sumer (located on the site of modern Iraq), promised compensation for those who were injured while working. Ur's laws date back to approximately 2000 BCE. Other ancient cultures had similar measures in place, many calling for precise payments for injuries to specific body parts. Even eighteenth-century pirates—those rough-and-tumble, pillaging prowlers of the sea—received predetermined compensation for the injuries they frequently received during battle. The loss of an eye or a finger would "earn" a pirate one hundred pieces of eight, the day's Spanish dollar. Compensation for the loss of limbs depended on which one was lost. The left leg was worth four hundred pieces of eight, while the right was worth five hundred. The left arm was five hundred pieces of eight, and the right arm was worth six hundred. In addition to the money, pirates received primitive substitutes for their missing limbs, often devised from a spare plank from the ship they were sailing on. Injured pirates also were assigned other jobs on the ship which did not require the use of the lost or maimed body part.

Governments eventually replaced all ancient compensatory practices and began implementing rules that were more restrictive. Under the common law that ruled in England from roughly the twelfth to the seventeenth centuries, three basic principles were used to determine whether an injured worker deserved to be compensated by his or her employer. Those principles included the following:

- **Contributory negligence**, or the principle that if a worker was in any way responsible for his injury, he would not receive any compensation.

Upton Sinclair and *The Jungle*

Written in 1906 by novelist Upton Sinclair, *The Jungle* is set in Chicago's meatpacking plants and stockyards at the turn of the twentieth century. While the book's main characters are fictional, the horrific and unsanitary conditions Sinclair describes were quite real at the time.

Chicago in the early 1900s was the center of America's meat industry. Its meatpacking district was almost a square mile in size, and some of the largest meat companies in the country were centered there. Some, including Armour and Swift, still are in business.

Sinclair wrote *The Jungle* as the result of an assignment from *Appeal to Reason*, a popular socialist newspaper. Socialists believe that workers, not investors, should own factories and the goods they produce. The Socialist movement was allied with labor union organizers early in the twentieth century, since the groups found common ground in the desire to improve conditions for workers.

Sinclair had been a writer and supporter of socialism since his teenage years in the early 1890s. For his research on *The Jungle*, he spent seven weeks in Chicago walking around the stockyards, talking to workers, and observing the operation of the meatpacking plants.

He saw extremely unsanitary conditions, employees who were worked at higher and higher speeds, with no time off, until they fell ill or died, and small children made to work in dangerous areas in and around machinery where an adult could not fit. Benefits of any kind were unheard of. In one of the book's more horrible stories, a worker falls into a vat of animal parts and is ground up along with the ingredients already there; his remains, like those of the animals, are sold as lard.

While Sinclair's intent was to attract more people to socialism, the effect of the novel on the American public was to move people to call for close inspection of the sanitary and working conditions in the meatpacking industry. The controversy led to the passage by Congress of the Pure Food and Drug Act of 1906 and also led to the establishment of the Food and Drug Administration in 1930. The federal agency is still in charge of food and medicine safety.

Upton Sinclair died in Arizona in 1968, at age ninety. He had written more than eighty books but still is and likely always will be best remembered for *The Jungle* and its lasting impact on food safety in America.

The Chicago meatpacking factories became notorious with the publication of *The Jungle*, by Upton Sinclair. Reforms that protected workers and consumers resulted from the outcry produced by his novel.

Government Entitlements

- **The "fellow servant" rule**, which disqualified workers from receiving any compensation if their injury was in any way caused by another worker.
- **The assumption of risk**, which basically represented acknowledgment that workers who take jobs in dangerous workplaces know they may be injured before they agree to work there. Oftentimes, employers made new employees sign contracts saying they would not sue the company if they were injured on the job.

These three principles were so favorable to employers that it was rare for workers get any compensation for on-the-job injuries. Injured workers' only resort—at least those who had not signed contracts foreclosing this possibility—was to sue their employers in court, an option too costly for most to pursue.

In 1871 Germany laid the groundwork for many modern-day workers' compensation programs with the creation of its limited Employers' Liability Law. Nine years later, England followed suit with a similar act, which was repealed in 1897 and replaced with the Workingmen's Compensation Act.

Across the Atlantic Ocean in the United States, the first workmen's compensation law was the Federal Employers' Liability Act (FELA), passed by Congress in 1908. Signed into law by President Theodore Roosevelt, the act was extremely limited in scope: it covered only railroad workers who were injured on the job. But FELA was a step toward the achievement of compensation rights for all injured workers, of whom there were many. In the year FELA was signed into law, 281,645 workers were injured on the job in the United States, and roughly 12,000 people were killed at work. These accidents helped create pressure for the enactment of wider-reaching laws to protect workers.

A number of states did not wait for the federal government to act and instead addressed the matter of workers' compensation in

The Triangle Shirtwaist Fire

The day after New York's workers' compensation law was ruled unconstitutional, one of the worst tragedies in American history struck the state's biggest city.

On March 25, 1911, five hundred Triangle Shirtwaist Company workers reported to work at the factory located on the top three floors of the Asch Building in Manhattan. The company made women's blouses, which were in those days called shirtwaists. Most of the workers were young women, many of them immigrants, and some only fifteen years old.

Around 4:40 p.m. a fire broke out in a cotton scrap bin on the eighth floor. Since enforcement of the regulations regarding fire escapes and emergency exits was lax, panicked workers on the ninth and tenth floors who tried to escape the flames found themselves trapped by malfunctioning elevators and pounding on locked doors. Company owners later explained the locked doors by asserting that the employees had been stealing material. Some of the workers on the ninth floor ventured onto a fire escape, only to have it bend and almost collapse under their weight—and the bottom foothold of the fire escape was far short of reaching the ground.

Firemen arrived on the scene quickly, but their ladders were too short to reach the people trapped on the ninth and tenth floors, and there was not enough pressure in the fire hoses to get water to the upper floors of the building.

In all, more than 140 of the workers were killed, many choosing to jump out the windows to avoid burning to death. Scenes of horror were recalled by witnesses in the city newspapers for weeks. One of the witnesses was Frances Perkins, who was to become secretary of labor in the cabinet of President Franklin Roosevelt. Describing that awful afternoon years later in a lecture at Cornell University, she said that the experience was the impetus for her career as an advocate for labor.

The tragedy created a national outcry for closer regulation of working conditions in America and prompted thousands of workers to join and support unions. Even the most conservative national commentators called for reforms.

Because there was no workers' compensation law, twenty-three of the victims' families had to sue for compensation for the loss of their family members. Two years after the fire, the owners of the Triangle Shirtwaist Company, who had already been acquitted of wrongdoing in a criminal trial, settled—for $75 per death.

Workers' Compensation

their own legislatures. One such law appeared on the books in New York in 1910, although it was ruled unconstitutional the following year. In that year, 1911, Wisconsin adopted a workmen's compensation law that granted both pay and medical coverage to injured workers. To secure passage of the law, however, its supporters had to compromise by striking from the draft bill language granting workers the right to sue their employers. That compromise was called the Great Trade-Off.

Shortly after Wisconsin's law hit the books, several more states enacted workers' compensation laws. The last state to enact an ongoing compensation law was Mississippi, which delayed until 1948. Every state now operates a no-fault system in which an employee can secure benefits simply by proving that the injury was work-related. But employees who accept benefits forfeit the right to sue.

Today, each state has control of its workers' compensation program. Individual companies set up their own programs through their insurance providers. A company pays a monthly premium to its provider, which in turn handles any claims the company may make. The exact amount of money a worker can expect to receive for the loss of an eye, a finger, an arm, or a leg is often predetermined. The rates vary from state to state. In Iowa, for example, workers can expect to receive 60 weeks of benefits for the loss of a thumb, but only 20 weeks of benefits for the loss of a pinkie finger. Loss of an entire hand qualifies the worker for 190 weeks' worth of benefits, while the loss of hearing in both ears qualifies a worker for 175 weeks.

An injured worker who files a workers' compensation claim faces a tedious process. But completing each step is important to receiving a favorable outcome. After being injured on the job, a worker typically notifies a supervisor and completes the appropriate claim forms. The next step is a visit to a doctor to have the injury examined and treated. Often, the employer arranges the appointment with one of the company's preferred doctors. At other

Government Entitlements

A worker who is injured on the job and can prove it will usually be eligible for workers' compensation benefits.

Workers' Compensation

times, the worker's own doctor will be consulted. Of course if the injury requires emergency treatment, medical help is most often sought first, and the claim forms are filed later.

The decision of whether to accept or deny a worker's claim rests in the hands of a claims administrator, who generally works for the employer's insurance company. If the claim is accepted, medical care for the injury will be paid for and the worker becomes eligible for payments to cover lost wages. The exact process varies from state to state. If the employer is self-insured, it pays. If the employee's company is not self-insured, coverage comes from a premium the employer pays to the state. If the claim is denied, the worker may appeal. It is customary to obtain the services of an attorney specializing in workers' compensation cases to assist in preparing an appeal. Employers are not allowed to punish workers who have filed such a claim by firing, discriminating against, or demoting them.

Injured workers can be awarded either temporary or permanent disability, depending on the severity of the injury. The amount of the benefits varies among states: in California and Florida, for example, the benefit rate is two-thirds the amount of a worker's wages before the injury. In addition, dependent children and spouses of workers who are killed on the job are eligible for payments called death benefits. Death benefits also vary from state to state, but are based on the worker's wages. They are paid monthly to the spouse, until he or she remarries, and to dependent children up to a certain age.

The current workers' compensation system in the United States is far from foolproof; indeed, it is riddled with fraud. In 2000 the National Insurance Crime Bureau reported that workers' compensation insurance fraud was the fastest-growing insurance scam in the nation, costing insurers an estimated $5 billion a year. District attorneys in the state of California prosecuted more than a thousand cases of fraudulent claims during the fiscal year 2007–2008, and 527 people were convicted of the crime, which is a felony in that state. In

Government Entitlements

one case from November 2009, a Vacaville woman was sentenced to nine months in jail and ordered to pay $66,117.57 in restitution, the exact amount she had been found guilty of defrauding.

Workers have various ways of trying to scam the system. Oftentimes, they exaggerate their symptoms or claim the injuries still cause problems long after the symptoms have disappeared. Reporting a non-work-related injury as having occurred on the job is another type of fraud, as is simply reporting injuries that never occurred. Some people who are receiving workers' compensation payments take other jobs but neglect to report the wages. Employers look for several telltale signs to determine what claims might be fraudulent. Examples include a lack of witnesses to the injury, employees who were not happy with their job prior to claiming to be injured, and employees who miss appointments with their doctors.

Fraud originates from all occupations, and even some whose sworn duty it is to uphold the law have been found guilty. In one high-profile case from March 2010, a Boston police detective who once had received a national award for his work in law enforcement was charged with thirty-four counts of fraud. Charging documents said the veteran officer, Eliezer Gonzalez, who had claimed a back injury, was photographed walking and acting normally, but when he showed up for his medical appointments, he was "walking slowly with the assistance of a cane and accompanied by associates who assisted him. . . . Gonzalez fraudulently acted both physically and mentally impaired, often requiring his associates to speak to the medical staff on his behalf." If he is convicted at trial, Gonzalez could receive a twenty-year prison sentence, followed by three years of supervision upon his release. The maximum monetary fine for each count of fraud is $250,000, which would add up to $8.5 million for Gonzalez.

Workers are not the only ones who commit workers' compensation fraud. Employers do it, too, most frequently by manipulating their financial records in order to lower their insurance premiums.

Workers' Compensation

Even health care providers sometimes participate in workers' compensation fraud. Some providers bill for services they did not perform, or order unnecessary tests to inflate the amount they receive from the employer's insurance company.

The many opportunities for fraud comprise one of the main complaints about workers' compensation programs. But, as entitlement programs go, workers' compensation is commonly thought of as one of the most effective in existence today.

During the eighty-seventh Veterans Day Parade in New York City, people lined the streets to show their support.

6 Veterans Affairs

ON THE LAST MONDAY IN MAY EVERY YEAR, cemeteries across the country fill with flower- and flag-bearing patriots who visit the gravesites of those who have served in America's military.

> The 30th day of May, 1868, is designated for the purpose of strewing with flowers, or otherwise decorating the graves of comrades who died in defense of their country during the late rebellion [the Civil War], and whose bodies now lie in almost every city, village and hamlet churchyard in the land. In this observance no form of ceremony is prescribed, but posts [veterans' organizations] and comrades will in their own way arrange such fitting services and testimonials of respect as circumstances may permit.

One day in each November, flags fly from homes in cities big and small and parades honor those who have served in the military, both living and dead.

> Now, Therefore, I, Dwight D. Eisenhower, President of the United States of America, do hereby call upon all of our citizens to observe Thursday, November 11, 1954, as Veterans Day. On that day let us solemnly remember the sacrifices of all those who fought so

Government Entitlements

valiantly, on the seas, in the air, and on foreign shores, to preserve our heritage of freedom, and let us reconsecrate ourselves to the task of promoting an enduring peace so that their efforts shall not have been in vain.

Americans did not need the national holidays of Memorial Day or Veterans Day, established in 1868 and 1954, respectively, to recognize how important a role their military personnel have played in the shaping of the country. As far back as 1636, the pilgrims of the Plymouth Colony in what is now Massachusetts had procedures in place for taking care of soldiers injured while defending the colony. The pilgrims, whose relations with the Pequot Indians were often hostile, created a law that guaranteed lifelong care to any soldier injured in battle.

In 1811 Congress passed an act that called for the building of "a permanent asylum for disabled and decrepit navy officers, seamen and marines." That home, located in Philadelphia, was the first federal medical facility exclusively for veterans. Today there are more than a hundred such facilities dedicated to caring for veterans and serving their families. Shortly after the Philadelphia home was commissioned, the government greatly expanded benefits for veterans and their families. Many of those homes were created in the years immediately following the American Civil War, which brought about numerous additional changes in the way America treated its veterans.

In 1862 the General Pension Act provided pension payments to disabled Union troops based on rank and disability. Confederate veterans did not receive any benefits. Many of the changes were necessitated by the sheer number of soldiers who fought in the war. Prior to the Civil War, there were only an estimated 80,000 veterans in the United States. At the end of the war in 1865, almost 2 million Union veterans were eligible for assistance. As a result, the government spent more on veterans' benefits from 1866

U.S. Naval Asylum and Hospital

In 1811 Congress passed an act calling for the building of "a permanent asylum for disabled and decrepit navy officers, seamen and marines." That home, the first federal medical facility exclusively for veterans, was located in Philadelphia. An "asylum" in those days was not a home for mentally challenged people; instead, the word meant "refuge," as in the modern sense of sanctuary for people who seek asylum in another country when threatened by a tyrannical government in their homelands.

The Naval Asylum building in Philadelphia was originally a country home owned by the wealthy Pemberton family. The Navy bought the property in 1826 and used the house both as the asylum and as a hospital for seven years, until a new building could be constructed. The new building, named Biddle Hall after one of the first administrators of the facility, housed the asylum, a hospital, and the first training academy for U.S. naval officers. The academy was moved to its present site in Annapolis, Maryland, in 1845, partly to relieve crowding in the asylum, where residents had been forced to live four to a room.

In 1848 the roof of Biddle Hall was raised to accommodate a new floor, which provided more space for retired and injured naval veterans. Major expansion of facilities was deemed necessary during the Civil War, however. Aware that a large influx of wounded sailors had overcrowded the hospital wing, Congress approved an additional building promptly, but the freestanding hospital was not completed until 1868.

In 1889 Biddle Hall was renamed as the U.S. Naval Home, and it remained a retirement facility for navy veterans until 1976, when a new naval home was opened in Gulfport, Mississippi. The old buildings, which still stand at Gray's Ferry Avenue and Twenty-fourth Street in Philadelphia, were sold in 1988 to private developers, who renovated the properties and turned them into condominiums.

to 1870 than it had in the previous seventy-five years. Subsequent laws broadened the benefits extended to veterans.

The massive numbers of American troops injured or killed during World War I prompted additional changes in the way the country dealt with its veterans, and in 1930 a single agency was created to oversee veterans' care. It was called the Veterans Administration but today, is known as the Department of Veterans Affairs (VA).

More American troops than ever before were called upon to fight in World War II. Shortly before the war ended in 1945, more than 400,000 American soldiers had been killed, more than 600,000 had been injured, and 12 million were about to be demobilized, at which point they would be unemployed. Many would need help readjusting to civilian life. The government subsequently enacted many new programs to address the situation. The groundwork for one such program actually had been laid a year earlier. It was called the Servicemen's Readjustment Act of 1944, more commonly known as the GI Bill of Rights, or GI Bill for short.

The GI Bill—which almost failed to pass because of a controversy related to a twenty-dollar weekly unemployment stipend—offered federal aid to veterans in such areas as hospitalization, home purchases, and most notably, education. Upon signing the bill on June 22, 1944, President Franklin D. Roosevelt said, "It gives servicemen and-women the opportunity of resuming their education or technical training after discharge, or of taking a refresher or retrainer course, not only without tuition charge up to $500 per school year, but with the right to receive a monthly living allowance while pursuing their studies." Specifically, the act covered tuition, books, and living expenses for veterans who decided to enroll in college or vocational schools. Before the benefits from the GI Bill ceased to be offered, in 1956, nearly 8 million veterans had applied those benefits to their education or training, and nearly 2.4 million home loans had been granted to veterans. Future legislation extended the benefits offered in the original GI Bill to cover more

Government Entitlements

The group of University of Iowa war veteran students facing the camera represent the 52 percent of those polled who said they would have attended college even without the GI Bill, and those with their backs turned represent the 48 percent who said they would not have been able to do so.

Veterans Affairs

veterans, even those who had served in times of peace. In 1984 the GI Bill was reworked and became known as the Montgomery GI Bill, after the man responsible for the updating, a former congressional representative named Gillespie V. "Sonny" Montgomery. In 2009 the Post–9/11 GI Bill became an educational-financing option for veterans who met certain criteria, which included serving after September 11, 2001, the date on which terrorists hijacked four planes and crashed them on American soil, killing nearly three thousand people.

Today, veterans' benefits are managed by individual states. Men and women who have been discharged from active service with the Air Force, Army, Coast Guard, Marine Corps, or Navy are eligible for most benefits, as are those who served as commissioned officers of the National Oceanic and Atmospheric Administration or its predecessor, the Environmental Science Services Administration, or the U.S. Public Health Service. The main benefit programs include the following:

- **Disability compensation**. These tax-free benefits are paid to veterans who were injured or contracted a disease while on active duty. The severity of the disability is ranked on a comprehensive percentage scale, and payments are made accordingly. In 2010 a single veteran without children who was declared 50 percent disabled received $770 per month. If the same person had been declared 100% disabled, he or she would have received $2,673 per month. The number of people in the disabled veteran's family also factors into the payment scale, as the amount of compensation goes up with each additional family member.
- **Education programs**. These include the Post–9/11 GI Bill, the Montgomery GI Bill, and the Reserve Education Assistance Program, which is available to National

The Impact of 9/11 on Social Welfare

Volumes have been written about the events of September 11, 2001: the horror of the worst terrorist attack in U.S. history, the loss of roughly three thousand American lives, the destruction of the World Trade Center and the damaging of the Pentagon, and the valor shown by the passengers who helped divert their hijacked United Airlines plane, and the first responders and the people of New York City in dealing with the attacks.

But 9/11 had more long-lasting effects, particularly with regard to social programs involving assistance for the families of those who died, and police, firefighters, and others who were killed, injured, or acquired health problems because of the attacks. Various programs also were created to assist those whose businesses or personal property was negatively affected by the events.

When the World Trade Center towers fell, for example, massive amounts of dust and dirt particles were flung into the air, and the firefighters and other emergency workers who responded to give aid to victims and search for survivors were at great risk of lung damage and other ailments from breathing the smoke and chemicals, as well as from physical contact with these materials.

Residents of New York and New Jersey, as well as some communities as far away as Connecticut and Pennsylvania, were affected by the cloud of dust and debris, which was large enough to be visible from space.

The state of New York and the federal Centers for Disease Control and Prevention set up a program for aid workers and volunteers who were affected while working at Ground Zero, the site of the destroyed towers. In addition to providing care for physical ailments, the World Trade Center Medical Monitoring and Treatment Program helps people who experienced unhealthy mental conditions, such as post-traumatic stress disorder and panic disorder, as a result of the attacks.

Several federal programs were set up after 9/11, to aid firefighters and other government workers injured in the rescue effort.

The U.S. Department of Justice also set up a special fund to pay cash to the families of people killed in all four crashes, as well as to those rescue workers and volunteers who were injured in the events. The 9/11 Victim Compensation Fund was funded by the federal government, and operated from 2001 through 2004.

The American Red Cross also has been involved in caring for the victims and families of 9/11, as have a number of private charities. Some have set up scholarship programs for the children of victims, while others perform such services as assisting with burial costs for people who die from 9/11-related causes.

As time has passed, most of the programs and funds that arose to cover the immediate and direct expenses of the victims have closed. Some, such as the World Trade Center Medical Monitoring and Treatment Program, will likely be around for decades to come, as survivors of the attacks, and the aid workers and volunteers who helped them, continue to deal with long-term medical issues.

Veterans Affairs

Guardsmen and Reservists who were called or ordered to a war or national emergency. Under the Post–9/11 GI Bill, veterans are eligible for payments for tuition and fees, a monthly housing allowance, and an annual book stipend. Exact amounts received vary greatly from state to state, but tuition costs, for example, average thousands of dollars per term.

- **Free or low-cost medical care.** Care is granted through roughly 1,400 VA hospitals and medical facilities located across the United States. Each veteran who enrolls in the VA health program is assigned to a priority group, which determines eligibility for benefits, as well as the amount of any copayments. Free care is automatically granted to former prisoners of war, those whose medical problems may be related to exposure to the herbicide Agent Orange or radiation from nuclear testing, those eligible for Medicaid, and those sixty-five years old or older.

- **Pension programs.** To be eligible for pension benefits, veterans must have served in the military for a predetermined amount of time, with at least one day of that service coming during war time. Veterans also must be permanently and totally disabled, must be sixty-five years old or older, and must have an annual income less than a set amount. For a veteran with no dependents, that amount is $11,830 per year. Monthly pension payments are based on how far below the set limit the veteran's annual income is. For example, if a veteran with no dependents made $10,000 in a year, his yearly pension amount would be $1,830, or $152.50 a month. Veterans who have received the Medal of Honor, awarded for extraordinary feats of valor, receive a pension payment in the amount of $1,194 per month.

Government Entitlements

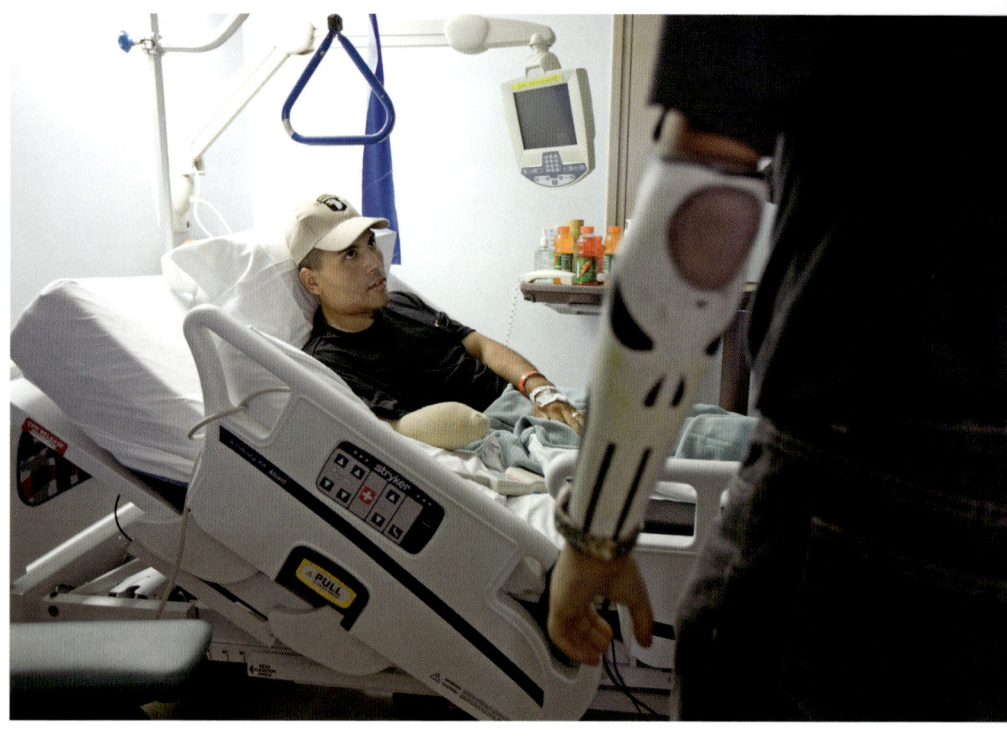

Very few people oppose medical benefits for wounded soldiers. Veterans' hospitals are often in the forefront of new medical technology as a result.

Other VA benefit programs include burials and memorials, counseling, home improvements designed to accommodate a veteran's disability, home loans, free prosthetics, and job training. Over the years, the home loans have helped millions of veterans buy their first homes. All VA programs are funded by the federal government.

As might be expected, criticisms of benefit programs for veterans are less numerous than those of perhaps any other form of entitlement. It is hard to dispute the appropriateness of providing basic necessities and quality medical care to those who have served their country. But there is some criticism of VA programs, much of it involving health care. In one recent high-profile case, many veterans' hospitals—including Walter Reed Army Medical Center in Washington, D.C., which traditionally was well respected for its state-of-the-art services—were investigated because of allegations of serious improprieties in patient care. Mental health experts also frequently call for more emphasis on the treatment of post-traumatic stress disorder, a condition often developed by people who, for example, have had terrible experiences in combat or have witnessed tragedy while participating in the treatment of battlefield injuries.

Veterans' benefits, or more specifically, the *funding* of such benefits, also is a hot-button topic for many. Such benefits come from the nondefense discretionary portion of the federal budget, which uses money the government has borrowed. The implications of borrowing money to pay for current services are vast and complex, and they impact every American citizen, with or without the individual's awareness.

7 Miscellaneous Entitlement Programs

NUMEROUS GOVERNMENT ENTITLEMENT PROGRAMS, for one reason or another, fall below the radar of most citizens. Many supplement better-known programs, especially welfare, but rarely make headlines and are not hotly debated on television talk shows, on websites, or in the newspapers. But that does not make them any less important to the millions of Americans who benefit from them each year. Several such programs stand out.

Social Services Block Grants

Funds from the Social Services Block Grant (SSBG) program are distributed on an annual basis to states to use as they see fit to run social service programs for their citizens. Such services might include help with day-care expenses, the prevention of child abuse, family planning, and additional help for the elderly and the disabled. In fiscal year 2010, a total of $1.7 billion was allotted for the program. The amount each state receives from that fund is based on its population. The heavily populated state of New York, for example, received $108 million during fiscal year 2010, whereas sparsely populated Alaska received just $3.8 million. The SSBG program, which is described in Title XX of the Social Security Act, was created in 1975 and amended in 1981 to include the block grants.

Miscellaneous Entitlement Programs

Foster Care and Adoption Assistance

Title IV of the Social Security Act created many social programs, including welfare itself, more formally known today as Temporary Assistance to Needy Families. The focus of Title IV's Part E, however, is a bit more specific: it provides funds to states for use in foster care and adoption assistance programs. Unlike the Social Services Block Grant program, Part E places no cap on the amount of money states can receive for services. The total expenditure in any given year depends on the number of children in need of assistance.

Foster father Stephen McCall brings a fast-food meal to his foster child Maleek. McCall became a foster parent of four children. In New York City alone, more than 25,000 children are in foster care.

Government Entitlements

Housing Assistance

Federal housing assistance programs reflect the belief that all Americans deserve a safe and affordable place to live. Such programs got their start during the Great Depression, when many families were struggling to find or maintain homes. Today, numerous programs exist to help low-income individuals searching for a place to live. Federal assistance options offered by the U.S. Department of Housing and Urban Development include public housing, the Housing Choice Voucher Program (widely known as Section 8), and Section 202.

Administered by local public housing agencies, housing choice vouchers can be used to cover the rent of apartments, town homes, and single-family residences, if the landlord agrees to accept the vouchers and the dwelling itself meets the program's requirements in terms of health and safety. A landlord who is willing to participate in the voucher program will be reimbursed by the government on behalf of the family.

Section 202 is for low-income elderly age sixty-two and above, and provides them places where they can live independently, yet also receive support as necessary with transportation, as well as cooking, cleaning, and other activities of daily living.

Farm Subsidies

One of the more controversial entitlement programs involves the giving of federal funds to farmers to help support their agricultural businesses. In times of a shortage of a particular crop, farmers may be paid to grow more of that crop, whereas in times of surplus, farmers might be paid to not grow a given crop. The farm subsidy system raises questions in the area of fair market competition. Why should one group of farmers receive subsidies when another does not? This topic is especially controversial in relation to considerations of rich versus poor countries. Rich countries, such as the United States, have the funds to supplement farmers' incomes to help keep costs of

Miscellaneous Entitlement Programs

Farm subsidies have been in place for decades. Here, Randy Floyd, the recipient of subsidies totaling more than $250,000 in five years, stands on his farmland.

Government Entitlements

their goods low, thus benefiting low-income grocery shoppers. Because poor countries lack such funds, however, their farmers must charge higher prices for their livestock and produce, which means that fewer people will be able to afford these foods.

Earned Income Tax Credit (EITC)

The Earned Income Tax Credit (EITC)—also known as the Earned Income Credit, or EIC—is a federal program administered by the Internal Revenue Service. It offers tax credits to low-income families. The program is especially helpful to families with children. Founded in 1975, the program is one of the largest entitlement programs in terms of monetary costs, yet many do not even think of its benefits as an entitlement. The program works by giving a predetermined tax break to low-income individuals, who enter a claim for the EITC on their tax forms. As a result, many are allowed to deduct a certain amount from their taxes. If a qualifying person's credit is high enough, however, he or she will receive money from the government instead of paying taxes.

Children's Health Insurance Program (CHIP)

The Children's Health Insurance Program (CHIP) is available to serve children in families who cannot afford private health insurance even though the parents make too much money to qualify for Medicaid and do not have access to such insurance from their employer. The program was created in 1997 as part of an amendment to the Social Security Act and reauthorized in 2009. CHIP operates similarly to Medicaid, in that individual states run their own programs based on federal guidelines. As such, specific provisions often vary from state to state, but all states offer basic medical coverage for low or no premiums and/or small copayments. Some states even use their CHIP funds to help adults in need. In 2008 there were 7.4 million children in the United States enrolled in

Miscellaneous Entitlement Programs

the program. That year, some 334,616 adults also received medical coverage from CHIP funds.

Child and Adult Care Food Program (CACFP)

Each day, roughly 3 million children across the United States receive meals, thanks to the U.S. Department of Agriculture's Child and Adult Care Food Program (CACFP). The program works by reimbursing approved, licensed day care centers for a percentage of what they paid for meals they provided to children. The program is administered by individual states.

Head Start

The national Head Start program was created in 1965 to prepare preschool children from low-income families for the dozen or more school years that lie ahead. The program offers federal grants to local organizations, which in turn provide educational, health, nutrition, and social programs to qualified children. Head Start is an extremely popular program that has helped more than 25 million preschool-age children since its inception. On average, the government spends $7 billion per year on the program.

Additional federal entitlement programs include school lunch and breakfast programs, energy-assistance programs, and job training programs for youth and adults.

8 Conclusion

THE DEBATE RAGES ON.

As long as there are government entitlement programs, Americans will continue to argue about them. Should they exist at all? Should some be cut or modified? Should all such programs be eliminated entirely, sending America back to its earliest days, when self-sustenance and the help of a neighbor were all one had to get by? Or should more entitlement programs be added?

The answers are never black and white.

The ever-changing nature of such programs is one reason for this, as is the issue of how wide-ranging the programs should be and, ultimately, who will pay for them. The health care reform bill of March 2010 shows exactly how much flexibility can be asked of entitlement programs. The reform, signed into law by Democratic President Barack Obama, requires all Americans to have health insurance coverage or face fines based on income level. It also requires businesses with more than fifty employees to offer medical coverage to those workers or pay fines for not doing so, makes changes to the Medicaid and Medicare programs, and offers federal subsidies to help low- to middle-income families obtain health insurance.

Opponents of the new law, who include Republican attorneys general of several states, have filed lawsuits asking the courts to declare the bill unconstitutional. Simon Lazarus, an attorney with the National Senior Citizens Law Center in Washington, D.C., says that if those legal challenges are successful, although he does

Conclusion

President Barack Obama, surrounded by lawmakers and honored guests, signed the Health Care Reform Act into law on March 23, 2010.

Government Entitlements

not believe they will be, they could lead to the dissolving of the Medicare, Medicaid, and Social Security programs. "The people who are challenging the constitutionality of the mandate [to obtain health insurance] are people who believe that Medicare and Social Security ought to be unconstitutional also," says Lazarus. "The arguments they're making would certainly call those programs into question. You couldn't really challenge this program without throwing some question over Medicare and Social Security."

At its most basic level, the debate on government entitlement begins with the question of whether the U.S. government should be involved at all in maintaining the social welfare of its citizens. Prior to the Great Depression and the ensuing New Deal, government involvement in social welfare issues was minimal. That is not the case today. In 2010 government entitlement programs accounted for almost 60 percent of federal spending. This spending—on programs such as Social Security, Medicare, and Medicaid—is categorized as "mandatory" in the yearly budget, which means that it must be distributed without debate. And the costs of entitlement programs are expected to continue to grow. Social Security costs, for example, are expected to rise from their 2010 price tag of $581 billion to $966 billion—written out, that is $966,000,000,000—in 2018, thanks to the retirement of massive numbers of baby boomers.

Those high financial costs of entitlement programs are another problem many people have. Randy Forbes, a Republican congressman from Virginia, likens government entitlement spending to a family budget gone out of control. In 2008 he wrote:

> [T]ake a piece of paper and tear off two-thirds of the paper. This is the proportioned amount of federal spending that automatically goes towards programs like Medicare, Medicaid, and Social Security. Now take a look at the remaining one-third of the piece of paper.

Conclusion

This is the amount we have left to cover our nation's entire spending on defense, health and scientific research, education, transportation, the environment, and all other requirements set forth in the Constitution. . . . Runaway entitlement spending is forcing us to attempt to fund everything else in our country on one-third of our budget, which is impossible. Just as if you attempted to spend two-thirds of a family budget on a mortgage payment, and use only one-third of the family budget to cover everything else the family must pay for like gas, college tuition, bills, health care, groceries, a car, and clothing, the likely result would be insurmountable debt. Likewise, the result of such a federal budget is a $9 trillion-and-growing deficit. This type of budgeting doesn't make sense for an individual family, and it doesn't make sense for our federal government.

Forbes's solution—and the solution offered by many other conservatives—is to remove the "mandatory" tag from entitlements and allow Congress to regularly review all such programs and make cuts or additions, as necessary, to help keep the programs in check in relation to the overall budget. This would allow the government more flexibility in terms of trying to balance America's budget. A balanced budget—which exists only when the amount of money coming in equals the amount going out—is important for many reasons. Most importantly, it helps keep the country out of debt, which is the result of borrowing, and requires paying interest on top of the original loan amount. Debt also burdens future generations that did nothing to incur the original debt.

Whether Forbes and those who share his views are right or wrong is of little or no concern to Americans of low incomes who are benefiting from such entitlement programs. Does a seventy-four-year-old woman on Social Security using battery-powered

Government Entitlements

lights around her home to trim electrical costs really care about balancing the federal budget? Does a mother of three in her late-thirties, who uses Medicaid to help cover the high medical costs of raising her disabled seven-year-old son worry about what will happen if that federal budget is not balanced?

But balances are indeed important, whether one is talking about the current federal budget or the obligations a civilized society has toward its citizens versus assuring that those obligations are capable of being met for both today *and* for the future. That future presents certain challenges, and determining exactly what, if any, changes should be made to government entitlement programs is one of them. The direction government entitlement programs take lies in the hands of politicians. Conservatives argue that entitlements undermine family values, create dependency, and cost too much. Liberals argue the opposite. Ultimately, the fate of those politicians, and the entitlement programs they debate, lies in the hands of voters: the common folk who use such programs, as well as those who do not and grumble about having to pay for them. Ultimately, it is up to the people.

Notes

Introduction

p. 5, "Caryn Elaine Johnson dropped out . . .": Laura B. Randolph, "The Whoopi Goldberg Nobody Knows," *Ebony*, March 1991, 111.

p. 5, "By eighteen, she was a . . .": Randolph, "The Whoopi Goldberg Nobody Knows," *Ebony*.

p. 6, "She told *Ebony* magazine in 1991 . . .": Randolph, "The Whoopi Goldberg Nobody Knows," *Ebony*.

p. 6, "The welfare system works . . .": Quoted in "Goldberg, Kennedy Oppose Republicans' Welfare Proposal," *Jet*, December 25, 1996, 33.

pp. 6–7, "In 2003, speaking in the U.S. House of Representatives…": Ron Paul, "Oppose the Federal Welfare State," February 13, 2003, www.lewrockwell.com/paul/paul80.html (accessed on December 12, 2009).

p. 7, "I have sometimes doubted whether the laws . . .": Quoted in June Axinn and Herman Levin, *Social Welfare: A History of the American Response to the Need* (New York: Longman, 1997), 27.

Chapter 1

p. 9, "One particularly gruesome text . . .": Ralph Dolgoff and Donald Feldstein, *Understanding Social Welfare* (Boston: Pearson Education, 2003), 21.

Government Entitlements

p. 9, "In the eighteenth century BCE. . . .": Richard Hooker ed., "The Code of Hammurabi," Washington State University: World Civilizations, www.wsu.edu/~dee/MESO/CODE.HTM (accessed October 15, 2009).

p. 10, "Islam's Prophet Muhammad said . . .": Quoted in Vincent J. Cornell, *Voices of Islam: Voices of Tradition* (Westport, CT: Praeger, 2007), 18.

p. 10, "Judaism teaches that . . .": Walter I. Trattner, *From Poor Law to Welfare State: A History of Social Welfare in America* (New York: Free Press, 1999), 3.

p. 10, "Christianity, which today has more adherents . . .": Dolgoff and Feldstein, *Understanding Social Welfare*, 27.

pp. 10–11, "Years of disease, famine, social instability, and wars . . .": Amanda Smith Barusch, *Foundations of Social Policy* (Itasca, IL: F. E. Peacock, 2003), 89.

p. 12, "Food in Jamestown was scarce . . .": "A Brief History of Jamestown," Jamestown-Yorktown Foundation, www.historyisfun.org/History-Jamestown.htm (accessed March 10, 2010).

p. 12, "However, the majority of the English . . .": Dolgoff and Feldstein, *Understanding Social Welfare*, 61.

p. 12, "that each towne shall provide . . .": Axinn and Levin, *Social Welfare*, 13.

p. 12, "In 1687, for example, one Massachusetts . . .": Trattner, *From Poor Law to Welfare State*, 18.

pp. 12, 14, "In one instance, that meant . . .": "Authentic Record of an Auction of the Poor," www.poorhousestory.com/AUCTION_POOR.htm (accessed December 22, 2009).

p. 14, "Author Walter I. Trattner writes . . .": Trattner, *From Poor Law to Welfare State*, 22–23.

p. 14, "In Massachusetts in 1860 . . .": "Trattner, *From Poor Law to Welfare State*, 59.

p. 17, "In most of the American colonies . . .": Axinn and Levin, *Social Welfare*, 28–29.

Notes

p. 17, "American Indians, whom the English settlers . . .": Trattner, *From Poor Law to Welfare State*, 23–24.

p. 20, "In 1790, the first year of the U.S. Census . . .": "First Census of the United States," www2.census.gov/prod2/decennial/documents/1790b-02.pdf (accessed December 21, 2009).

p. 20, "But just ten years later . . .": "1800 Census," www.1930census.com/1800_census.php (accessed December 22, 2009).

p. 20, "By 1900, there were more than . . .": "1900 Census," www.1930census.com/1900_census.php (accessed December 22, 2009).

p. 20, "In 1800, the average American died . . .": "National Vital Statistics Reports: United States Life Tables 2003, www.cdc.gov/nchs/data/nvsr/nvsr54/nvsr54_14.pdf (accessed December 22, 2009).

p. 29, "Within three years, roughly one out of every four . . .": Robert Van Giezen and Albert E. Schwenk, "Compensation from before World War I through the Great Depression," Bureau of Labor Statistics, January 30, 2003, www.bls.gov/opub/cwc/cm20030124ar03p1.htm (accessed December 23, 2009).

pp. 30–31, "For so long as man has lived on this earth . . .": John T. Woolley and Gerhard Peters, *The American Presidency Project Online*. www.presidency.ucsb.edu/ws/?pid=26452 (accessed December 24, 2009).

p. 32, "By 1974, the national poverty rate . . .": Dolgoff and Feldstein, *Understanding Social Welfare*, 95–96.

p. 32, "During his 1992 presidential campaign, . . .": Adam Nagourney, "Clinton Proposes 2-Year Limit on Welfare," *USA Today*, September 10, 1992, A-12.

Chapter 2

p. 35, "An act to provide for . . .": "The Social Security Act of 1935: Preamble," Social Security Online, www.ssa.gov/history/35actpre.html (accessed December 23, 2009).

Government Entitlements

p. 36, "The worker, after years of productive effort . . .": "Social Security in America," Committee on Economic Security, www.ssa.gov/history/reports/ces/cesbook.html (accessed December 24, 2009).

p. 37, "A twenty-three-year-old businessman from New York . . .": "The First SSN & The Lowest Number," Social Security Online, www.ssa.gov/history/ssn/firstcard.html (accessed December 24, 2009).

p. 37, "According to the U.S. Social Security Administration . . .": "Historical Background and Development of Social Security," U.S. Social Security Administration, www.ssa.gov/history/briefhistory3.html, (accessed December 24, 2009).

p. 37, "In 1940, the first year . . .": "OASDI Benefits Awarded: Summary," "Annual Statistical Supplement to the Social Security Bulletin, 2009," February 2010, Social Security Administration, 6.3.

p. 38, "According to the *Los Angeles Times* . . .": Dennis McLellan, "Last-Known Civil War Widow Dies at 97," *Los Angeles Times*, June 1, 2004, dailyuw.com/2004/6/1/last-known-civil-war-widow-dies-at-97/ (accessed March 2, 2010).

p. 40, "In 1949 old-age assistance welfare programs . . .": Sylvester J. Schieber and John B. Shoven, *The Real Deal: The History and Future of Social Security* (New Haven, CT: Yale University Press, 1999), 89.

p. 40, "But, thanks to COLAs, . . .": "OASDI Benefits Awarded: Summary," "Annual Statistical Supplement to the Social Security Bulletin, 2009," February 2010, Social Security Administration, 6.3.

p. 40, "The 1975 amendment also established . . .": "Supplemental Security Income," U.S. Social Security Administration, www.ssa.gov/ssi/ (accessed on December 22, 2009).

p. 41, "Fuller paid a total of $24.75 . . .": "Details of Ida May Fuller's Payroll Tax Contributions," Social Security Administration, www.ssa.gov/history/idapayroll.html (accessed on March 10, 2010).

Notes

p. 42, "President Johnson, who believed Medicare to be a . . .": Barusch, *Foundations of Social Policy*, 63.

p. 44, "Initially, that resistance came from . . .": Barusch, *Foundations of Social Policy*, 64.

p. 44, "[I]f you don't [stop Medicare] . . .": Quoted in "House Democrats Expose Campaign of Misinformation on Health Insurance Reform," U.S. House of Representatives Committee on Education & Labor, July 31, 2009, edlabor.house.gov/newsroom/2009/07/house-democrats-expose-campaig.shtml (accessed on January 30, 2010).

p. 44, "Having given our pensioners . . .": Quoted in "House Democrats Expose Campaign of Misinformation on Health Insurance Reform," U.S. House of Representatives Committee on Education & Labor, July 31, 2009.

p. 47, "This bill demonstrates for all time …": Quoted in Schieber and Shoven, *The Real Deal*, 195.

p. 48, "Owing to the sheer numbers …": "A Summary of the 2009 Annual Reports," Social Security and Medicare Boards of Trustees, www.socialsecurity.gov/OACT/TRSUM/ (accessed on February 24, 2010).

p. 48, "In 1983 Social Security's trust fund . . .": Schieber and Shoven, *The Real Deal*, 197.

p. 48, "Medicare's current situation is almost . . .": "A Summary of the 2009 Annual Reports," Social Security and Medicare Boards of Trustees, www.socialsecurity.gov/OACT/TRSUM/ (accessed on February 24, 2010).

p. 48, "In 1950 there were sixteen . . .": "Ratio of Social Security Covered Workers to Beneficiaries," Social Security Online, www.ssa.gov/history/ratios.html (accessed on February 25, 2010).

p. 48, "When the Social Security Act was . . .": "Estimated Life Expectancy at Birth in Years, by Race and Sex," February 18, 2004, Centers for Disease Control and Prevention, www.cdc.gov/nchs/data/dvs/nvsr52_14t12.pdf (accessed on December 23, 2009).

Government Entitlements

p. 48, "Thanks to advances in . . .": "U.S. Life Expectancy Hits a New High of 78," Reuters, August 19, 2009, www.reuters.com/article/idUSTRE57I6BF20090820 (accessed February 25, 2010).

p. 49, "That is a fact Beverly Nash . . .": Bob Moos, "Dollar Wise: Seniors Offer Model for Getting By through Frugality," *Dallas Morning News*, February 15, 2009, www.dallasnews.com/sharedcontent/dws/dn/latestnews/stories/DNseniorsurvivors_15bus.ART.State.Edition1.4c56eef.html (accessed on February 10, 2010).

p. 49, "Karen Raymond was sixty-six years old . . .": Liz Pulliam Weston, "Could You Survive on Social Security?" MSN, March 22, 2007, articles.moneycentral.msn.com/RetirementandWills/PlayingCatchUp/CouldYouSurviveOnSocialSecurity.aspx (accessed on January 12, 2010).

p. 50, "In January 2010, more than 52 million people . . .": "Monthly Statistical Snapshot: January 2010," U.S. Social Security Administration Office of Retirement and Disability Policy, January 2010, www.socialsecurity.gov/policy/docs/quickfacts/stat_snapshot/#table2 (accessed on March 10, 2010).

p. 50, "Yet even though most people . . .": "The Coming Entitlement Meltdown," Ron Paul, March 6, 2007, www.lewrockwell.com/paul/paul372.html (accessed on March 2, 2010).

Chapter 3

p. 53, "It's just a social message . . .": Quoted in Jill Duerr Berrick, *Faces of Poverty: Portraits of Women and Children on Welfare* (New York: Oxford University Press, 1995), 106.

pp. 53–54, "As evidence, she cites . . .": Berrick, *Faces of Poverty*, 11.

p. 54, "The monthly payout was $18 . . .": "A Brief History of the AFDC Program," U.S. Department of Health & Human Services, aspe.hhs.gov/hsp/afdc/baseline/1history.pdf (accessed on March 10, 2010).

Notes

p. 54, "The program was described as a defensive measure . . .": Axinn and Levin, *Social Welfare*, 191.

p. 56, "Author Berrick describes the shift . . .": Berrick, *Faces of Poverty*, 9.

p. 56, "Those coupons, or food stamps, . . .": "The Food Stamp Act of 1964," U.S. Department of Agriculture, August 31, 1964, www.fns.usda.gov/FSP/Rules/Legislation/history/PL_88-525.htm (accessed on January 15, 2010).

p. 58, "Thirty-seven-year-old Sheri Stapler . . .": Author interview, March 27, 2010.

p. 61, "Included among those initially eligible were . . .": "Tracing the History of CMS Programs: From President Theodore Roosevelt to President George W. Bush," Centers for Medicare and Medicaid Services, www.cms.hhs.gov/History/Downloads/PresidentCMS-Milestones.pdf (accessed on January 10, 2010).

p. 61, "Those requirements are broken up into . . .": "Medicaid At-a-Glance 2005," Centers for Medicare & Medicaid Services, www.cms.hhs.gov/MedicaidEligibility/Downloads/Medicaidata-Glance05.pdf (accessed on January 10, 2010).

p. 62, "But, according to at least one study . . .": Barusch, *Foundations of Social Policy*, 134.

p. 63, "No longer were those receiving . . .": "Major Provisions of the Personal Responsibility and Work Opportunity Reconciliation Act of 1996," Department of Health and Human Services, April 28, 1997, library.findlaw.com/1997/Apr/28/130301.html (accessed on January 12, 2010).

p. 64, "In the 1970s alone . . .": *2004 Green Book*, U.S. House of Representatives Ways and Means Committee, August 4, 2004, frwebgate.access.gpo.gov/cgi-bin/getdoc.cgi?dbname=108_green_book&docid=f:wm006_08.pdf (accessed on January 17, 2010).

p. 64, "In 2002, some $20 billion . . .": *2004 Green Book*.

Government Entitlements

p. 66, "WIC participants receive monthly checks . . .": "WIC: The Special Supplemental Nutrition Program for Women, Infants and Children," U.S. Department of Agriculture, November 2009, www.fns.usda.gov/wic/WIC-Fact-Sheet.pdf (accessed on February 25, 2010).

p. 67, "I looked both of these women . . .": Star Parker, *Pimps, Whores and Welfare Brats: From Welfare Cheat to Conservative Messenger* (New York: Pocket Books, 1997), 12.

Chapter 4

p. 69, "For the past 4 years the American people . . . .": Stanley King, December 1933 issue of *American Labor Registration Review*, reproduced in *Unemployment Compensation: What and Why?, Social Security Board*, March 1937, www.larrydewitt.net/SSinGAPE/UI-1937book2.htm (accessed on February 12, 2010).

p. 70, "The United States began to consider . . . ": First Annual Report of the Nebraska Unemployment Compensation Division, February 1, 1938, 5–6.

pp. 70, 73, "[T]he distress of the masses . . .": "The Struggle of the Unemployed," Communist League of Struggle, May 1935, www.weisbord.org/Unemployed.htm (accessed on January 3, 2010).

p. 73, "By 1935, unemployment levels . . .": Van Giezen and Schwenk, "Compensation from Before World War I through the Great Depression" *Compensation and Working Conditions*, Fall 2001, www.bls.gov/opub/cwc/cm20030124ar03p1.htm#37 (accessed on February 12, 2010).

p. 76, "The federal Extended Unemployment Compensation Act . . .": Barusch, *Foundations of Social Policy*, 58–59.

p. 76, "In California, as of January 2010 . . .": "Unemployment Insurance Statistics," California Employment Development Department, www.edd.ca.gov/About_EDD/Quick_Statistics.htm#UIStatistics (accessed March 15, 2010).

Notes

p. 76, "Some economic studies suggest . . .": Casey B. Mulligan, "Do Jobless Benefits Discourage People from Finding Jobs?" *The New York Times*, March 17, 2010, economix.blogs.nytimes.com/2010/03/17/do-jobless-benefits-discourage-people-from-finding-jobs/?src=tptw (accessed on March 18, 2010).

p. 77, "Doesn't create new jobs. . .": Ryan Grim, "GOP Sen. Kyl: Unemployment Benefits Make People Not Want to Get a Job," *The Huffington Post*, March 1, 2010, www.huffingtonpost.com/2010/03/01/gop-sen-kyl-unemployment_n_481526.html (accessed on March 10, 2010).

p. 78, "Economist Bruce D. Meyer . . .": David R. Francis, "Unemployment Insurance," Library of Economics & Liberty, 2002, www.econlib.org/library/Enc1/UnemploymentInsurance.html (accessed on March 10, 2010).

p. 79, "In 2009, a period of atypically high unemployment . . .": Unemployment Compensation: Federal-State Partnership, U.S. Department of Labor, Office of Employment Insurance, October 2009, workforcesecurity.doleta.gov/unemploy/pdf/partnership.pdf (accessed on February 5, 2010).

p. 79, "In November 2007, the U.S. unemployment rate . . .": "Focus on Economic Data: U.S. Employment and the Unemployment Rate," Council for Economic Education, March 2010, www.econedlink.org/lessons/index.php?lesson=749&page=teacher (accessed on March 21, 2010).

Chapter 5

p. 81, "A 23-year-old male was . . .": Kathleen Moreo, "Workers' Compensation Case Study—Then and Now," PRIME Education, April 4, 2007, primeinc.org/casestudies/casemanager/study/478/Workers_Compensation_Case_Study_--_Then_and_Now (accessed on March 2, 2010).

127

Government Entitlements

p. 82, "The laws of Ur . . .": Samuel Noah Kramer, *History Begins at Sumer* (London: Thames & Hudson, 1958), 93.

p. 82, "Even eighteenth century pirates . . .": "Injury Compensation," Piratesinfo.com, July 9, 2006, www.piratesinfo.com/cpi_Injury_Compensation_537.asp (accessed on January 2, 2010).

pp. 82, 86, "Under the English common law . . .": Gregory P. Guyton, "A Brief History of Workers' Compensation," *The Iowa Orthopaedic Journal*, 19 (1999), www.ncbi.nlm.nih.gov/pmc/articles/PMC1888620/#R4 (accessed on February 12, 2010).

p. 86, "In the year FELA was signed . . .": "Federal Employers' Liability Act (1908)," *Major Acts of Congress*, ed. Brian K. Landsberg, Macmillan-Thomson Gale, 2004, www.enotes.com/major-acts-congress/federal-employers-liability-act (accessed on March 10, 2010.)

p. 88, "Scenes of horror were recalled . . .": Leon Stein, *The Triangle Fire* (New York: Carroll & Graf/Quicksilver, 1962), 54–55.

p. 88, "One of the witnesses was Frances Perkins . . . ": "Lecture by Frances Perkins," September 30, 1964, www.ilr.cornell.edu/trianglefire/texts/lectures/perkins.html (accessed on February 16, 2010).

p. 88, "Two years after the fire . . .": Frequently Asked Questions," Iowa Workers' Compensation Commissioner, www.iowaworkforce.org/wc/faq.htm#Frequently (accessed on January 15, 2010).

p. 91, "In 2000 the National Insurance Crime Bureau . . .": "Fraud: Workers' Compensation Fraud and Convictions," California Department of Insurance, 2010, www.insurance.ca.gov/0300-fraud/0100-fraud-division-overview/0500-fraud-division-programs/workers-comp-fraud/index.cfm (accessed on February 22, 2010).

pp. 91–92, "In one case from November 2009 . . .": "November 2009 Workers' Compensation Fraud Convictions," California Department of Insurance Fraud Division," www.insurance.ca.gov/0300-fraud/0100-fraud-division-overview/0500-fraud-division-programs/workers-comp-fraud/upload/November2009.pdf (accessed on February 22, 2009).

Notes

p. 92, "In one high-profile case from March 2010, . . .": David Abel and Maria Cramer, "Officer indicted on fraud charges," *Boston Globe*, March 25, 2010, www.boston.com/news/local/massachusetts/articles/2010/03/25/detective_indicted_on_34_counts_of_fraud/?page=1 (accessed on March 26, 2010).

Chapter 6

p. 95, "The 30th day of May, 1868 . . .": "Memorial Day Order, General Orders No. 11," May 5, 1868, www.cem.va.gov/hist/memdayorder.asp (accessed on January 14, 2010).

p. 95–96, "Now, Therefore, I, Dwight D. Eisenhower . . .": Dwight D. Eisenhower, "Title 3—The President: Proclamation 3071," *Federal Register*, October 12, 1954, www1.va.gov/opa/vetsday/docs/proclamation_1954.pdf (accessed on January 14, 2010).

p. 96, "As far back as 1636 . . .": "VA History," U.S. Department of Veterans Affairs, March 9, 2010, www4.va.gov/about_va/vahistory.asp (accessed on March 15, 2010).

p. 76, "After the men signed up . . .": "Veterans Benefit History," PBS, May 13, 2005, www.pbs.org/now/society/vetbenefits.html (accessed January 14, 2010).

p. 96, "In 1862 the General Pension Act . . .": "Honoring the Call to Duty: Veterans' Disability Benefits in the 21st Century," Veterans Disability Benefits Commission, October 2007, 32–33.

p. 99, "Upon signing the bill on June 22, 1944 …": "Born of Controversy: The GI Bill of Rights," U.S. Department of Veterans Affairs, November 6, 2009, www.gibill.va.gov/GI_Bill_Info/history.htm (accessed on January 10, 2010).

p. 101, "In 2010 a single veteran without children . . .": "Veterans Compensation Benefits Rate Tables," U.S. Department of Veterans Affairs, December 1, 2009, www.vba.va.gov/bln/21/Rates/comp01.htm#BM02 (accessed on January 10, 2010).

Government Entitlements

p. 105, "Free care is automatically granted to . . .": Dolgoff and Feldstein, *Understanding Social Welfare*, 256.

p. 105, "For a veteran with no dependents . . .": "Veteran's Pensions," Military.com, www.military.com/benefits/military-pay/veterans-pensions (accessed on March 12, 2010).

p. 105, "Veterans who have received . . .": Department of Veterans Affairs, *Federal Benefits for Veterans, Dependents and Survivors* (Washington, DC: U.S. Government Printing Office, 2010), 35.

Chapter 7

p. 108, "In fiscal year 2010 . . .": "FY 2010 SSBG Allocations," U.S. Department of Health & Human Services, March 2, 2010, www.acf.hhs.gov/programs/ocs/ssbg/docs/esalloc10.html (accessed on March 20, 2010).

p. 112, "In 2008 there were 7.4 million . . .": "The Children's Health Insurance Program (CHIP)," Centers for Medicare and Medicaid Services, www.cms.hhs.gov/LowCostHealthInsFamChild/ (accessed on February 11, 2010).

p. 113, "Each day, roughly 3 million children . . .": "Child & Adult Care Food Program," U.S. Department of Agriculture," March 17, 2009, www.fns.usda.gov/cnd/Care/CACFP/aboutcacfp.htm (accessed on February 11, 2010).

p. 113, "Head Start is an extremely popular program . . .": "About NHSA," National Head Start Association, www.nhsa.org/about_nhsa (accessed on February 11, 2010).

p. 113, "On average, the government spends $7 billion . . .": "Head Start Program Fact Sheet," U.S. Department of Health & Human Services, February 2008, www.acf.hhs.gov/programs/ohs/about/fy2008.html (accessed on February 11, 2010).

Notes

Chapter 8

p. 116, "The people who are challenging . . .": Arthur Delaney, "*Successful Legal Challenge of Health Care Reform Could Topple Medicare, Social Security: Legal Expert,*" The Huffington Post, March 24, 2010, www.huffingtonpost.com/2010/03/24/successful-legal-challeng_n_511713.html (accessed March 25, 2010).

p. 116, "In 2010 government entitlement programs . . .": "Our View on the Federal Budget: You Can't Cut the Deficit without Touching Benefits," *USA Today*, January 25, 2010, blogs.usatoday.com/oped/2010/01/debate-on-the-federal-budget-our-view-you-cant-cut-the-deficit-without-touching-benefits.html (accessed on March 12, 2010).

pp. 116–117, "[T]ake a piece of paper and tear off . . .": Randy Forbes, "The Challenge of Giant Entitlements," April 4, 2008, www.house.gov/forbes/newsroom/enewsletter/2008/04042008.htm (accessed on March 12, 2010).

Further Information

Further Reading

Beland, Daniel. *Social Security: History and Politics from the New Deal to the Privatization Debate*. Lawrence: University Press of Kansas, 2005.

Hays, Sharon. *Flat Broke with Children: Women in the Age of Welfare Reform*. New York: Oxford University Press, 2003.

Santow, Leonard J., and Mark E. Santow. *Social Security and the Middle Class Squeeze: Fact and Fiction about America's Entitlement Programs*. Westport, CT: Praeger, 2005.

Wallace, Douglas. *Everything Will Be All Right: A Memoir*. Austin, TX: Greenleaf Book Group Press, 2010.

Whitney, Catherine. *Soldiers Once: My Brother and the Lost Dreams of America's Veterans*. Cambridge, MA: Da Capo Press, 2009.

Worth, Richard. *Social Security Act*. New York: Marshall Cavendish Benchmark, 2010.

Further Information

Websites

Social Security Online

www.ssa.gov

The official website of the U.S. Social Security Administration includes a detailed history of the program, as well as information about Medicare.

U.S. Department of Veterans Affairs

www.va.gov

Offers a comprehensive look at nearly every aspect of concern to veterans; includes a history of the program, current news updates, and more.

Bibliography

Abel, David, and Maria Cramer. "Officer Indicted on Fraud Charges." *Boston Globe.* March 25, 2010.

Axinn, June, and Herman Levin. *Social Welfare: A History of the American Response to the Need.* New York: Longman, 1997.

Barusch, Amanda Smith. *Foundations of Social Policy.* Itasca, IL: F. E. Peacock, 2003.

Berrick, Jill Duerr. *Faces of Poverty: Portraits of Women and Children on Welfare.* New York: Oxford University Press, 1995.

Chambers, Donald E. *Social Policy and Social Programs: A Method for the Practical Public Policy Analyst.* Boston: Allyn & Bacon, 2000.

Cornell, Vincent J. *Voices of Islam: Voices of Tradition.* Westport, CT: Praeger, 2007.

Dolgoff, Ralph, and Donald Feldstein. *Understanding Social Welfare.* Boston: Pearson Education, 2003.

Bibliography

Grim, Ryan. "GOP Sen. Kyl: Unemployment Benefits Make People Not Want to Get a Job." *The Huffington Post*, March 1, 2010.

Guyton, Gregory P. "A Brief History of Workers' Compensation," *The Iowa Orthopaedic Journal*, 1999.

Jansson, Bruce S. *The Reluctant Welfare State*. Stamford, CT: Wadsworth Brooks/Cole, 2001.

Kramer, Samuel Noah. *History Begins at Sumer*. London: Thames & Hudson, 1958.

McLellan, Dennis. "Last-Known Civil War Widow Dies at 97." *Los Angeles Times*, June 1, 2004.

Moos, Bob. "Dollar Wise: Seniors Offer Model for Getting By through Frugality." *The Dallas Morning News*. February 15, 2009.

Mulligan, Casey B. "Do Jobless Benefits Discourage People from Finding Jobs?" *New York Times*, March 17, 2010.

Nagourney, Adam. "Clinton Proposes 2-Year Limit on Welfare." *USA Today*, September 10, 1992, A-12.

Parker, Star. *Pimps, Whores and Welfare Brats: From Welfare Cheat to Conservative Messenger*. New York: Pocket Books, 1997.

Randolph, Laura B. "The Whoopi Goldberg Nobody Knows." *Ebony*, March 1991.

Government Entitlements

Schieber, Sylvester J., and John B. Shoven. *The Real Deal: The History and Future of Social Security.* New Haven, CT: Yale University Press, 1999.

Stapler, Sheri. Author interview. March 27, 2010.

Stein, Leon. *The Triangle Fire.* New York: Carroll & Graf/Quicksilver, 1962.

Trattner, Walter I. *From Poor Law to Welfare State: A History of Social Welfare in America.* New York: Free Press, 1999.

Index

Page numbers in **boldface** are photographs.

Addams, Jane, 26, 27–28
Aid to Dependent Children (ADC), 54-55
Aid to Families with Dependent Children (AFDC), 5, 32, **52**, 55, 63, 66
almshouses, 14, 15–16
American colonies, needy in, 11-20
American Indians, 17
American Red Cross, 104
assumption of risk, 86

baby boom generation, 47, 48
balanced U.S. budget, 117–118
Biddle Hall, 97, 98
Black Americans, 17, 53, 55
boom vs. bust times, 21
Buddhism, 10

Bush, George H.W., 46
Bush, George W., 44

categorically needy, 61, 62
Centers for Medicare and Medicaid Services (CMS), 61
charitable societies, 23
Child and Adult Care Food Program (CACFP), 113
Child Care and Development Fund (CCDF), 64-66
Children's Bureau, federal, 26
Children's Health Insurance Program (CHIP), 112–113
child support, 64-66, **65**
civil rights movement, 55
Civil War, 21, **22**, 95, 98
Civil War Pension program, 38, 96
Clinton, Bill, 32, 63
contributory negligence, 82

Government Entitlements

copayment, 43, 105, 112
cost-of-living adjustment (COLA), 40

Darwin, Charles, 22, 23, 24–25
death benefits, 91
demographic change, 20–21, 55–56
dependency, cycle of, 7, 23, 32, 66, 118
deserving poor, 11, 56
disabilities, 46, 108
  Medicaid and, 61, 62
  pirate's compensation, 82
  Social Security, 38, 40, 42
  temporary/permanent, **90**, 91
  veterans, 101, 105–106

early-retirement, 42
Earned Income Tax Credit (EITC), 112
Economic Opportunity Act, 30, 32
Egyptian welfare aid, 9
Eisenhower, Dwight D., 95
elderly, 21, 108
  housing assistance, 110
  Medicaid and, 62
  Medicare and, 42–43
  pensions, 30, 36–39, 72
electronic benefit transfer cards (EBTs), 58, 60

Employers' Liability Law, Germany, 86
energy assistance program, 113
English common law, 82
English Poor Laws, 9, 11, 12, 17
entitlement programs, 8, 9
  benefits, 6
  cost of, 7, 116, 117, 118
  debate over, 114, 116
  defined, 5
Environmental Science Services Administration, 101

fair market competition, 110
farm subsidies, 110, **111**, 112
federal block grant program
  TANF, 63
  WIC, 66
Federal Deposit Insurance Corporation, 72
Federal Emergency Relief Administration, 29
Federal Employers' Liability Act (FELA), 86
Federal Insurance Contributions Act (FICA), 36, 51
Federal Office of Child Support Enforcement, 64
fellow servant rule, 86
Five Pillars of Islam, 10

138

Index

flop houses, 70
Food and Drug Administration, 84
food stamp, **4**, 32, 56–58, **57**
   evolution of, 59-60
   fraud, 58
   funding cuts, 46
   surplus food and, 59–60
Food Stamp Act, 56
foster care and adoptive assistance, 109, **109**
Foster Care Program, 26
Franklin, Benjamin, 7, 17, 18–19, 66
fraud
   food stamp, 58
   Medicaid, 62
   workers' compensation, 91–93
Freedmen's Bureau, 21–22
French and Indian War, 20, 21
Fuller, Ida May, 41

general assistance program, 80
General Pension Act, 96
GI Bill of Rights, 99–101, **100**
Goldberg, Whoopi, **4**, 5, 6
Goldwater, Barry, 44
Gonzalez, Eliezer, 92

Great Depression, 29–30, 46, 49, 59, 69, 70, 72–75, **75**, 80, 110, 116
Great Recession, 79–80, **79**
Great Society, 56
Great Trade-Off, 89

Hammurabi's code of laws, 9
Head Start, 32, 113
Health Care Reform Act (2010), 114, **115**
health insurance, federal, 42
Hinduism, 10
Hoover, Herbert, 29, 72
Hospital Insurance Trust Fund, 48
housing assistance, 110
Housing Choice Voucher Program, 110
Hull House, 26

immigrants, 17, 20, 63, 87
indentured servants, 12–14, **13**
industrialization, 21, 26
inflation, 45

Jamestown settlement, 11, 12
job training programs, **31**, 32, 113
Johnson, Lyndon B., 30–32, **31**, 42, 44, 55, 56

139

Government Entitlements

The Jungle, 83, 84, **85**
  See also Sinclair, Upton

Kennedy, John F., 30, 56

labor unions, 83, 88
life expectancy, 20–21, 48

meatpacking industry, 83–**85**
Medicaid, 32, 42, 58, 61–63, 112, 116, 118
  eligibility categories, 61–62, 66
  funding, 46, 62
  health care reform and, 114
  veterans eligibility, 105
medically needy, 62
Medicare, 32, 42–44, 48, 50
  health care reform and, 114
  opposition to, 44, 45
  Part A, 43
  Part B, 43
  Part C (Medicare Advantage), 43
  Part D, 43, 44
Memorial Day, 96
minimum wage, 50
Montgomery, Gillespie V., 101
Montgomery GI Bill, 101
Moynihan, Daniel P., 55
Moynihan Report, 55
Muhammad, Islam's Prophet, 10

Nash, Beverly, 49
National Oceanic and Atmospheric Administration, 101
National Welfare Rights Organization, 55
natural selection, 23, 24–25
New Deal, 29–30, 32, 38, 72, 75, 116
9/11 terrorist attack, 102–104, **103**
9/11 Victim Compensation Fund, 104
no-fault system, 89

Obama, Barack, 51, 62, 114
Office of Economic Opportunity, 32
Office of Child Support Enforcement, 64
Old Age, Survivors, and Disability Insurance (OASDI), 35
on-the-job injuries, 86, 92
Owen, Grace D., 37

Parker, Star, 67
Paul, Ron, 6, 50
pay-go (paygo) system, 37, 48
pensions, 30, 44
  early-retirement option, 42
  history of, 38-42
  Social Security, 36–39
  veterans, 38, 96, 105
  work, 49

Index

Perkins, Frances, 88
personal identification number (PIN), 58
Personal Responsibility and Work Opportunity Reconciliation Act, 32
Pilgrims, 12, 96
poorhouse, 14, 15–16
　See also almshouses
Poor Law of 1601, 11
Post-9/11 GI Bill, 101, 105
post-traumatic stress disorder, 107
privatization, 50-51
Progressive Era, 26, 29–30
public housing, 110
　See also housing assistance
Pure Food and Drug Act, 84

Raymond, Karen, 49
Reagan, Ronald, 32, 44–**47**,
religions, charity and, 10
Reserve Education Assistance Program, 101, 105
Revolutionary War, 20, 21, 38
Roman *annona* program, 9
Roosevelt, Eleanor, 72
Roosevelt, Franklin, 29–30, 38, **39**, 47, **68**, 70–72, 75, 88, 99

Roosevelt, Theodore, 26, 86
school lunch and breakfast programs, 113
Servicemen's Readjustment Act of 1944, 99
settlement movement, 23, 26–27
Sinclair, Upton, 83–84, **85**
　See also *The Jungle*
single parent, 5–6, 26, 54–55, 64–65
Social Darwinism, 23, 25
socialism, **39**, 83–84
Social Security, 8, **34**, 82, 116–117
　COLAs, 40
　defined, 35
　eligibility, 42, 51
　life on, 49–50
　reserves, 48
Social Security Act (1935), 16, 30, 35–36, 38, **39**
　adjustments to (1977), 44, 47–49
　Aid to Dependent Children, 54–55, 59
　amendment (CHIP, 1997), 112
　amendment (COLAs, SSI, 1972), 40
　amendment (early retirement, 1961), 42

141

Government Entitlements

amendment (Medicare, 1965), 42, 61
amendment (1983), 47
funding, 37, 41
Title III (unemployment insurance), 69–80, 82
Title IV, Part E, 109
Title XX (SSBG), 108
Social Security Administration, 37, 38
Social Security card, 37–39
Social Security Disability Insurance (SSDI), 42
Social Security number, **34**, 37, 38, 39
Social Services Block Grants (SSBG), 108, 109
soup kitchens, **75**
Special Supplemental Nutrition Program for Women, Infants and Children (WIC), 66
Spencer, Herbert, 23
Stapler, Sheri and Randy, 58
Supplemental Security Income (SSI), 40, 42
Sweeney, John David Jr., 37

taxation, 7–8, 11, 112
for Medicare, 43, 44
payroll, 41, 43–44, 50–51, 73
for Social Security, 36

for unemployment insurance, 73
Temporary Assistance for Needy Families (TANF), 5, 32–33, 61, 63, 66
Triangle Shirtwaist Company fire, 87–88
Truman, Harry S., 40, 42

undeserving poor, 11, 56
unemployment, 45
in American colonies, 14
Great Depression, 29, 72–74, 80
Social Security and, 48
Works Projects Administration and, **68**
unemployment insurance (UI), 8, 69–80, 82
critics of, 76, 77–78
goal of, 76
Great Recession and, **79**
how it works, 73, 76
U.S. Constitution, Amendments, 26
U.S. Naval Asylum and Hospital, 96, 97
See also Biddle Hall
U.S. Public Health Service, 101
urbanization, 21
Ur's (Sumerian city-state) compensation laws, 82

Index

Veterans Administration, 99
veterans affairs, 95–107
 benefits (Civil War), 21, 38
 benefits (colonial), 17
 funding, 106, 107
 main benefits programs, 101, 105
 observances/parades, **94**, 95
 other benefit programs, 106–107
 Social Security and, 38
Veterans Affairs, Department of (VA), 99
Veterans Day, **94**, 95, 96
veterans hospitals, 106-107, **106**

Wallace, Alfred Russel, 24
War on Poverty, 30, **31**, 32, 55
Welfare Reform Act (1996), 32, 63
White House Conference on the Care of Dependent Children, 26
widows and orphans, 26, 54
 ADC, 54–55
 death benefits, 91
 survivor's benefits, 40
 of war, 20, 21
women in workforce, 55–56, 63

workers' compensation, 81–93
 in ancient cultures, 82
 basic principles, 82, 86
 claim procedure, 89, **90**, 91
 foreign laws, 86
 fraud, 91-93
Workingmen's Compensation Act, England, 86
Works Projects Administration (WPA), **68**
World Trade Center Medical Monitoring and Treatment Program, 103, 104
World War I, 29, 75, 99
World War II, 30, 45, 59, 72, 75, 99

About the Author

JEFF BURLINGAME is the award-winning author of roughly twenty books, including *The Lost Boys of Sudan* in our Great Escapes series and *Prisons*, in this series. In 2011, his book on Malcolm X was nominated for an NAACP Image Award for Outstanding Literary Work—Youth and Teens. Before becoming a full-time author, Burlingame was a writer and an editor for various newspapers and magazines. He resides with his family in Washington State.

Alpena Co. Library
211 N. First Ave.
Alpena, MI 49707